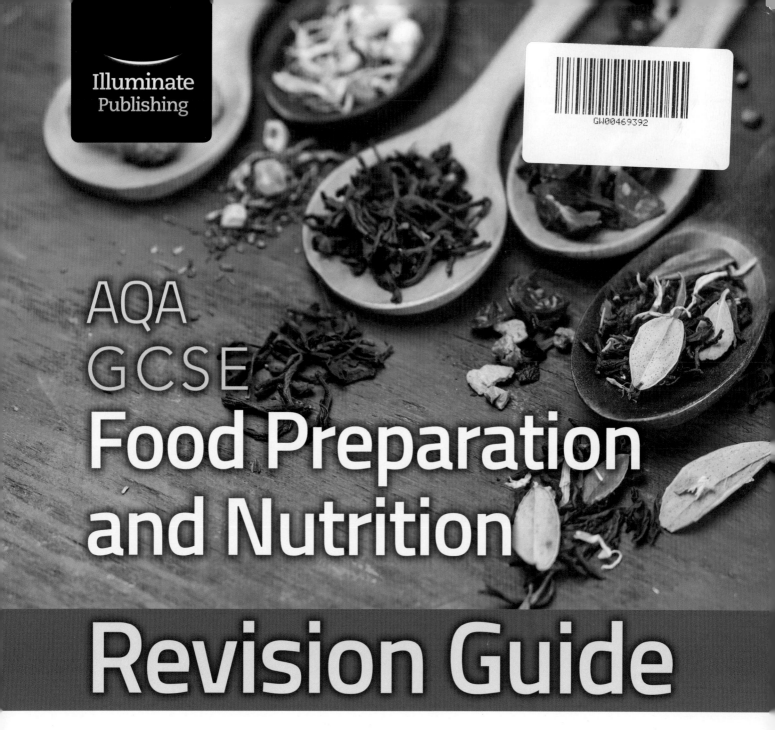

AQA
GCSE
Food Preparation and Nutrition

Revision Guide

Anita Tull

First published in 2017 by Illuminate Publishing Ltd, P.O. Box 1160, Cheltenham, Gloucestershire GL50 9RW

First printed 2017

Orders: Please visit www.illuminatepublishing.com
or email sales@illuminatepublishing.com

British Library Cataloguing in Publication Data

A catalogue record for this book is available from the British Library

ISBN 978-1-911208-80-2

Printed by Barley Print, Tuffley, Hertfordshire

04.17

The publisher's policy is to use papers that are natural, renewable and recyclable products made from wood grown in sustainable forests. The logging and manufacturing processes are expected to conform to the environmental regulations of the country of origin.

Every effort has been made to contact copyright holders of material reproduced in this book. If notified, the publishers will be pleased to rectify any errors or omissions at the earliest opportunity.

Editor: Geoff Tuttle

Design and layout: Nigel Harriss

Acknowledgements

Animation and film stills have been taken from *AQA GCSE Food Preparation and Nutrition: Digital Book Bundle* by Anita Tull *et al.* © Illuminate Publishing Ltd (p36, 37, 58, 59 61, 65, 77, 78, 87, 100, 112)

Other illustrations and photographs © Shutterstock.com

Contents

For answers to Activities and Stretch and Challenge questions visit
www.illuminatepublishing.com/aqafoodrganswers

Introduction

This revision guide has been produced to help you to prepare for the written examination that you will take in the final year of the GCSE Food Preparation and Nutrition course.

The written examination is worth **50%** of your final GCSE grade, and this guide will help you to plan your revision and achieve your potential.

The details of the written examination are:

> **Time allowed:** 1 hour and 45 minutes
>
> **Section A:**
> 20 multiple choice questions from all sections of the course:
> **20 marks**
>
> **Section B:**
> 5 questions of different styles from different sections of the course
> **80 marks**
>
> **TOTAL: 100 marks**
>
> All questions must be answered

Chapter 13 in the student textbook and Chapter 12 in this revision guide give you more information about the types of questions you may be asked to answer and provide revision tips and advice to help you.

In the written examination you will be tested on the five sections of the specification:

1. Food, nutrition and health
2. Food science
3. Food safety
4. Food choice
5. Food provenance

How to use this guide

This guide contains a range of features to help you to learn and revise the information you need to know for the written examination. Some of this information will also help with your non-examined assessment:

1 **Summaries of topics that are covered in your course**

- These are presented in note form in tables, charts and mind maps to help you remember the main information.

- Many images are included to help you visualise the information.

- Remember that each topic is linked to each of the five sections of the GCSE Food Preparation and Nutrition specification, and in your answers to exam questions, you will need to show your knowledge of how they are linked. Here is an example of how a topic is linked:

Revision tip

Key terms

Activity

Applying your learning:

THEORY INTO PRACTICE

Multiple choice challenge

Knowledge check

Stretch and challenge questions

2 Revision tips
- To give you some ideas and suggestions about different ways of revising.
- To give you some important reminders of how best to present the information in your answers.

3 Key terms
- These are to remind you of the key words / vocabulary and their meanings for each topic that you should try to include in your answers.

4 Activities
- A variety of activities, e.g. puzzles, charts to complete, quizzes, etc., to help you learn the topics and test your knowledge.

5 Revision mind maps
- Illustrated to help you remember key information.
- You can use these as a template to make your own mind maps to help you revise other topics.

6 Applying your learning
- Apply the information you have revised to a real-life situation.

7 Theory into practice – try a practical challenge
- Have a break from your desk and go into the kitchen and demonstrate what you know about a topic by making a recipe.
- Answer some questions about what you are making.
- As you work, think about how all the sections of the specification apply to the ingredients you are using in your recipe.

8 Practice examination questions
- Multiple choice questions – with spaces to fill in your answers.
- Knowledge check – can you recall? – Read about a topic then test yourself on key facts.
- Stretch and challenge questions – have a go at answering some types of questions that you will have to answer in Section B of the examination.

Answers are provided for Multiple Choice and Knowledge Check questions and can be found on pages 145–152.

For answers to Activities and Stretch and Challenge questions visit www.illuminatepublishing.com/aqafoodrganswers

Revision myths

'I will revise last minute'

Last minute cramming does work – ONLY if you have revised hard beforehand so that you can quickly retrieve the knowledge from your brain.

'I can't revise.'

Yes you can. It might be tricky and boring and hard – but everyone can do it, given the right strategies and with effort.

'My brother/sister/friend didn't revise and they got great grades.'

Nobody gets excellent results in examinations without effort. They may not be as visible, or they may have worked incredibly hard in lessons back when it was first learned, but those who do best revise.

'My friends aren't revising – they told me.'

Nobody goes around shouting about how hard they're working. We want it to look natural and we want to look like it is easy, but it almost always isn't. Don't believe them and get caught out!

'I don't know how to revise.'

Your school will give you lots of effective strategies. There are some included in this revision guide. Practise them – they work.

We hope that you find this guide useful.

Good luck with your written examination!

Chapter 1: Nutrients

Protein

Book-link:
1.1.1 Protein, pages 2–9

What do you need to know?

You need to know about the importance of **nutrients and water** for our health.

Nutrients are natural chemicals found in foods that are needed by the body for different reasons.

Next you need to know:

- The different nutrients: **Macronutrients** (protein, fat, carbohydrate)
  Micronutrients (vitamins, minerals)
- The **functions** of nutrients and water in the body (what they do)
- The main **sources** of nutrients and water (which foods they are found in)
- The effects of a **deficiency** (not enough) or excess (too much) of a nutrient and water on the body
- The **amount** of nutrients and water needed every day for different life stages

Key learning: PROTEIN

What you must know about protein	In your answers, you need to know how to explain:	Further information you can add to extend your answers:
What it is and what it is made of	• Protein is a **macronutrient** which is found in animal and plant foods • Protein molecules are made up of 'building blocks' called **amino acids**	• Proteins are very large molecules • There are at least **20 amino acids**
Why amino acids are important	• 10 amino acids are **essential** for children • 8 amino acids are **essential** for adults • **High biological value (HBV)** proteins contain all 10 **essential amino acids** • **Low biological value (LBV)** proteins are missing one or more **essential amino acids**	• We must get **essential amino acids** from the food we eat (other amino acids can be made in our bodies from protein foods we eat) • If you eat two or more **LBV protein foods** together you will get all the **essential amino acids** • This is called **protein complementation**: e.g. beans on toast, lentil soup and bread, rice and peas, nut butter on bread, rice and bean salad 

What protein does in the body (its functions)	Protein is needed for:
	• Body **growth**
	• **Repair** of the body when it is injured
	• Giving the body **energy**
		• Protein is needed by plants and animals
		• Children are growing so they need more essential amino acids than adults
		• The body will only use protein for energy if it does not have enough from carbohydrates and fats
		• Proteins are also needed to make other essential things, e.g.:
		  – hormones, e.g. to make you grow
		  – enzymes, e.g. to digest your food
		  – antibodies, e.g. to help you fight infections

Which foods give us protein (sources of protein)	**HBV protein foods:** meat, poultry, fish, eggs, milk, cheese, yogurt, quark, soya beans, quinoa **LBV protein foods:** beans, peas, lentils, cereals [rice, wheat, oats, barley, rye, millet, sorghum] and cereal products [bread, pasta, etc.], nuts, seeds, gelatine **Protein alternatives:** Made from soya: tofu, tempeh, textured vegetable protein Mycoprotein made from a high protein fungus, e.g. Quorn™	
What happens if you do not have enough protein (a deficiency)	• Children do not grow properly • Hair loss • Poor skin and nails • Infections • Poor digestion of food	• The body cannot grow without the right amount of protein • Hair is not essential so the body will stop it growing if it is short of protein • Skin and nails contain protein so will weaken without enough protein • The immune system needs protein to stop infections • The digestive system will not work properly without enough protein
What happens if you have too much protein	• Excess stored as fat • Weight gain – obesity • Puts a strain on the liver and kidneys	

Revision tip

To show your understanding of essential amino acids, HBV and LBV proteins and protein complementation, make sure you can give some examples of different foods in which they are found.

Key terms you should try to use in your answers

Amino acids: the 'building blocks' that join together to make protein molecules

Essential amino acids: amino acids that the body cannot make by itself and must get from the food we eat

Biological value: the number of essential amino acids that a protein food contains

Protein complementation: eating different LBV protein foods together in order to get all the essential amino acids that the body needs

Activity 1.1

Solve the puzzle below by filling in the missing letters. The clues are in the questions:

P _ _ _ _ _   is the group name for peas, beans and lentils, which are good sources of LBV protein

R _ _ _ _ _   of the body is one of the functions of protein

O _ _ _   and seeds are two LBV protein foods that are ingredients in muesli

T _ _ _   is one of three alternative protein foods beginning with a 'T' – (what are the other two?)

E _ _ _ _ _   protein is only used for this if the body doesn't have enough from carbohydrate or fat

I _ _ _ _ _ _ _ _ _   these will happen a lot if the body does not have enough protein

N _ _ _   these are good sources of LBV protein

Applying your learning

A 14-year-old friend has been in an accident and is recovering from a broken arm and cuts and grazing on their legs.

• Explain why it is important as they recover that they eat plenty of different foods containing protein.

• Which other nutrients will be particularly important to help their recovery? Give reasons for your answers.

THEORY INTO PRACTICE
– try this practical challenge

Plan and make a main course dish for your friends/ family that shows your understanding of protein complementation.

Carry out a nutritional analysis of the recipe you used.

QUESTIONS

Using your knowledge of nutrition and sustainability of food, answer these questions:

* Using your nutritional analysis to help you, explain how the ingredients in the recipe were used for protein complementation. *(2 marks)*

* Explain why LBV protein foods are usually cheaper to buy and have less of an impact on environmental sustainability than HBV protein foods. *(3 marks)*

Here is a revision mind map to help you learn about protein:

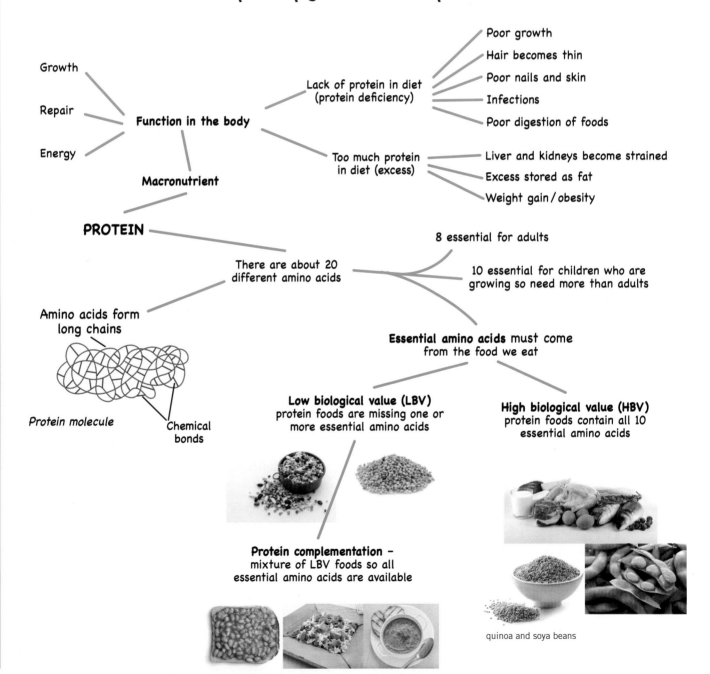

Growth

Repair

Energy

Function in the body

Macronutrient

PROTEIN

Lack of protein in diet (protein deficiency)

Poor growth
Hair becomes thin
Poor nails and skin
Infections
Poor digestion of foods

Too much protein in diet (excess)

Liver and kidneys become strained
Excess stored as fat
Weight gain / obesity

There are about 20 different amino acids

8 essential for adults

10 essential for children who are growing so need more than adults

Amino acids form long chains

Protein molecule   Chemical bonds

Essential amino acids must come from the food we eat

Low biological value (LBV) protein foods are missing one or more essential amino acids

High biological value (HBV) protein foods contain all 10 essential amino acids

Protein complementation – mixture of LBV foods so all essential amino acids are available

quinoa and soya beans

2 Fat

Book-link:
1.1.2 Fat, pages 10–16

Key learning: FAT

What you must know about fat

In your answers, you need to know how to explain:

Further information you can add to extend your answers:

What it is and what it is made of

- **Fat** is a **macronutrient** which is found in animal and plant foods
- **Fats** are solid at room temperature
- **Oils** are liquid at room temperature
- Fats and oils have the same structure and same **energy value**

- Fat / oil molecules are called **triglycerides**
- A triglyceride looks like this:

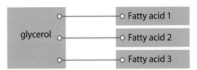

glycerol — Fatty acid 1 / Fatty acid 2 / Fatty acid 3

What fatty acids are

Types of **fatty acids**:

- **Monounsaturated** fatty acid: type of fatty acid found in solid fats and liquid oils
- **Saturated** fatty acids: found mainly in solid fats, e.g. butter, lard, suet, block vegetable fat, ghee, the fat in meat, palm oil, coconut and chocolate

  Unsaturated fatty acids: found mainly in liquid plant oils such as olive, rapeseed, sunflower and corn; and also oily fish, avocado pears, nuts, seeds and some vegetable fat spreads

What fat does in the body (its functions)

- Gives **energy** which is stored in the body
- 1g fat gives **9 kcals / 37 kJ**
- **Insulates** the body from the cold
- **Protects** bones and kidneys from physical damage
- Provides **vitamins A, D, E, K**

- Fat is stored mainly in **adipose tissue cells** under the skin
- Adipose tissue **insulates** the body from the cold and provides a 'cushion' to protect the bones and kidneys
- The body breaks down the fat stores to release **energy** if there is not enough available from carbohydrate
- Vitamins A, D, E and K are known as 'fat soluble' vitamins

Which foods give us fat (sources of fat)

- **Visible fats and oils:** fats / oils in a food that you can easily see: e.g. fat in meat, oil in tuna, butter, lard, suet, block vegetable fat, ghee, plant oils such as olive, palm, sunflower oil
- **Invisible fats and oils:** fats / oils in a food that you cannot easily see: e.g. in cakes, pastries, potato crisps, biscuits, chocolate, nuts, fried foods, meat products, etc.

- Foods containing fat are **energy dense**
- It is easy to consume a lot of energy from these foods without realising it as they are very palatable (tasty) and easy to eat

What happens if you do not have enough fat (a deficiency)

Rare in the UK, but deficiency causes:

- Weight loss
- Feeling cold
- Bruising of bones if knocked
- Lack of vitamins A, D, E, K

- The body prefers to use carbohydrate for energy
- If it does not have enough energy from food, the body will use up the stores of fat from adipose tissue and elsewhere in the body

What happens if you have too much fat	Common in the countries like the UK and causes: • Excess stored as body fat • Weight gain – obesity • Organs such as the liver store fat in them which stops them working properly • Can lead to coronary heart disease	• The body will store a lot of fat in adipose tissue cells • Excess fat is also stored elsewhere in the body, e.g. around the intestines, liver and other vital internal body organs, which puts a strain on them • Excess fat stores can lead to diseases such as obesity, Type 2 diabetes, heart disease, high blood pressure, shortage of breath
What is the recommended amount of fat per day	• The amount adults need is a % **of total daily energy intake** • Total fat: no more than **35%** of food energy per day	• **Saturated fats:** approximately **11%** of food energy per day • **Monounsaturated fatty acids:** approximately **13%** of food energy per day • **Polyunsaturated fats:** approximately **6.5%** of food energy per day

Revision tip

Make sure that you understand and can explain:

- Why foods containing fats and oils are energy dense.

- Why it is important to understand about visible and invisible fats and oils (and give examples of each).

Key terms you should try to use in your answers

Fat: a macronutrient that supplies the body with energy

Oils: fats that are liquid at room temperature (e.g. sunflower oil, olive oil)

Fatty acids: parts of a fat molecule

Triglyceride: a fat molecule made from 1 part glycerol and 3 fatty acids

Monounsaturated fatty acid: fatty acid found mainly in solid fats and liquid oils

Saturated fatty acids: fatty acids found mainly in solid fats

Unsaturated fatty acids: fatty acids found mainly in liquid oils

Visible fats: fats in a food that you can easily see (e.g. fat on meat, a block of butter)

Invisible fats: fats in a food that you cannot see because they are a part of the food (e.g. butter in cooked pastry, oils in fried foods such as potato crisps and chips)

Applying your learning

You are planning to make a cold (not baked) cheesecake as part of a meal for some friends. Two of your friends are trying to reduce their energy intake from food, so you want to reduce the energy density of the cheesecake recipe by changing some of the ingredients.

The ingredients for the cheesecake recipe are listed below:

- Explain which ones you would change and what you would use instead of them.

- Give reasons for your answers.

- Carry out a nutritional analysis to show how you have reduced the energy density in the recipe by making the changes.

Biscuit base:
250g digestive biscuits
100g butter

Filling:
150g cream cheese
300g condensed milk
150g double cream
Juice of 2 lemons

Top layer:
75g Lemon curd

Here is a revision mind map to help you learn about fat:

Keeps body warm (insulates body)

Protects bones and kidneys

Provides vitamins A, D, E, K

Energy store

Common in UK
Fats are energy dense
Weight gain
Obesity
Coronary heart disease

Too much fat (excess)

Rare in UK
Weight loss
Feeling cold
Bruising of bones if knocked
Lack of vitamins A, D, E, K

Lack of fat in diet (fat deficiency)

Functions of fat in the body

FAT

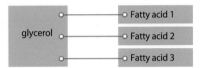

glycerol — Fatty acid 1 / Fatty acid 2 / Fatty acid 3

Fat molecule **= Triglyceride** — Macronutrient

Fats – **solid** at room temperature
Oils – **liquid fats** at room temperature

Visible fats / oils

Invisible fats / oils

Fatty acids are either:

Saturated   **Unsaturated**
(monounsaturated or polyunsaturated)

butter, ghee, lard, block vegetable fat, palm oil, coconut, chocolate, suet

oils – olive, rapeseed, sunflower; oily fish, avocado, nuts, seeds, vegetable fat spread

Animal: butter, lard, suet, fat on meat, ghee, cod liver oil, oily fish

Plant: white vegetable fat, cocoa butter, coconut cream, nut and seed oils

Animal: cheese, cakes, biscuits, pastries, sausages, salami, pies, ready meals, take away foods, milk, cream, ice cream egg yolk, oily fish

Plant: vegetable fat spread, chocolate, seeds, nuts, olives, avocados, fried foods, salad cream, mayonnaise, hummus, crisps, chips

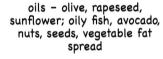

Activity 1.2

Look at the pictures in the chart below and identify which of the foods contain visible and/or invisible fat.

For each one you identify, explain why the fat it contains is visible and/or invisible:

Food	Visible fat? Invisible fat? ... or both?	Explain why you have given this answer

3 Carbohydrates

Book-link:
1.1.3 Carbohydrates, pages 16–21

Key learning: CARBOHYDRATES

What you must know about carbohydrates

In your answers, you need to know how to explain:

Further information you can add to extend your answers:

What they are and what they are made of	• Carbohydrate is a **macronutrient** which is found in plant foods	• Carbohydrate is made by plants during **photosynthesis**:

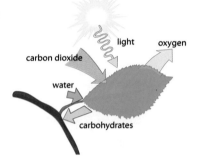

light, oxygen, carbon dioxide, water, carbohydrates

	• There are two groups of carbohydrates:
	  – sugars
	  – complex carbohydrates
		Sugars:
		
		• **Monosaccharides:** glucose, fructose, galactose
		• **Disaccharides:** sucrose, lactose, maltose
			Complex carbohydrates:
			
			• **Polysaccharides:**
			  – starch
			  – pectin
			  – dextrin
			  – dietary fibre (also called non-starch polysaccharide – NSP)
			  – glycogen (made by animals and humans in their bodies)

What carbohydrates do in the body (their functions)	• Main source of **energy** • Dietary fibre helps the body get rid of **waste products**	• **Glycogen** is stored in the liver and muscles for instant source of energy (e.g. running) • Carbohydrates are broken down in the body to **glucose** which is used by body cells for energy	
Which foods give us carbohydrates (sources of carbohydrate)	• **Glucose:** ripe fruits and vegetables (e.g. apples, onions, beetroot, parsnip, sweet potato) • **Fructose:** fruits, vegetables and honey • **Galactose:** milk from mammals • **Maltose:** barley, a syrup (malt extract), added to breakfast cereals, biscuits, hot drink powders, confectionery (sweets) • **Sucrose:** 'sugar' from sugar cane and sugar beet and used in cooking and many processed foods, drinks and confectionery • **Lactose:** milk and milk products • **Starch:** cereals (e.g. wheat, rice, oats, barley, maize [corn]), cereal products (e.g. breakfast cereals, pasta, bread, cakes, pastry, biscuits); starchy vegetables (e.g. potatoes, yams, sweet potatoes, parsnip, pumpkin, butternut squash, peas, beans, lentils); seeds, quinoa		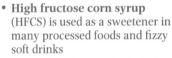• **High fructose corn syrup** (HFCS) is used as a sweetener in many processed foods and fizzy soft drinks • Sugars found naturally in fruits, vegetables and milk (not added to them) are **intrinsic sugars**

- **Pectin**: some fruits, e.g. oranges, lemons, oranges, limes, apples, apricots, plums, greengages and some root vegetables, e.g. carrots

- **Dextrin**: formed when starchy foods (e.g. bread, cakes, biscuits) are baked or toasted

- **Dietary fibre / Non-starch polysaccharide (NSP)**: wholegrain cereals and cereal products, e.g. breakfast cereals, bread

- Pasta, flour; fruits and vegetables, especially with skins left on (e.g. peas, beans, lentils); seeds, nuts

- **Free sugars** are released during food processing (e.g. fruit juices) or added to foods to sweeten them (e.g. honey, syrup, sugar used in cooking, concentrated fruit juice)

What happens if you do not have enough carbohydrate? (a deficiency)	• Rare in the UK and similar countries • Lack of energy, tiredness • Weight loss • Severe weakness • Not enough fibre – constipation	
What happens if you have too much carbohydrate	• Excess carbohydrate not used for energy is **stored as fat** • Weight gain – obesity	• Frequently eating too many **refined and processed carbohydrates** (e.g. white bread, doughnuts, biscuits, cakes, potatoes, white rice, pasta, etc.) and **free sugars** (e.g. sugar, sugary foods, sweet soft drinks, biscuits, cakes) can lead to: – Raised blood sugar levels – Type 2 diabetes – Tooth decay
What is the recommended amount of carbohydrate per day	• The amount we need is a % **of total daily energy intake** (from age 2 years upwards) • Sugar: **no more than:** – 4 tsp/day 4–6-year-olds – 5 tsp/day 7–10-year-olds – 6 tsp/day 11-year-olds – adults	• **Total carbohydrate: 50%** of food energy per day • **Free sugars**: no more than **5%** of total carbohydrate intake • **Dietary fibre (NSP)**: Adults: at least 30g a day Children: 2–5 yrs: 15g a day 5–11yrs: 20g a day 11–16 yrs: 25g a day 16–18 yrs: 30g a day

Revision tip

When answering a question about the effects of sugar on people's health, remember to show your understanding and knowledge of where sugars are found in different foods, and the different names that are used for them by food manufacturers on food labels, e.g. dextrose, malto-dextrin, fructose, high fructose corn syrup (HFCS).

Key terms you should try to use in your answers

Photosynthesis: the process where green plants trap energy from the sun and form carbohydrates

Sugars: a group of carbohydrates that taste sweet

Monosaccharides: a group of sugars that are made of one sugar molecule

Disaccharides: a group of sugars that are made of two sugar molecules

Polysaccharides (complex carbohydrates): a group of carbohydrates that are made from many sugar molecules joined together, but do not taste sweet

Activity 1·3

Solve the puzzle below by filling in the missing letters. The clues are in the questions:

C _ _ _ _ _ _   carbohydrates include starch, pectin and dietary fibre

A _ _ _ _ _ _ _ _   is a white starchy powder that is used to thicken liquids

R _ _ _   vegetables are a good source of starch

B _ _ _ _ _   is a cereal that is used to make maltose

O _ _ _ _ _ _   is a health condition that may develop if a person eats too much carbohydrate

H _ _ _   is the abbreviation for a substance that is used to sweeten many soft drinks and foods

Y _ _ _   are root vegetables that contain a lot of starch

D _ _ _ _ _ _   is formed when starchy foods are heated in an oven or under a grill

R _ _ _ _ _ _   as a sport needs a lot of glycogen to be stored in the leg muscles

A _ _ _ _ _ _ _   need to load their body with carbohydrates before an event

T _ _ _ _ _ _ _   is the name of a vitamin which helps to release energy from carbohydrates

E _ _ _ _ _   carbohydrates supply the body with most of this

S _ _ _ _ _   are the group of carbohydrates which includes galactose, fructose and sucrose

Applying your learning

Some teenagers are taking part in an athletics competition in a week's time and will be running in several races.

Explain why it is important that they eat plenty of foods containing carbohydrate in the next few days.

List a breakfast, lunch and evening meal that they could eat and give reasons for why these meals will help prepare their bodies for the competition.

Here is a revision mind map to help you learn about carbohydrate:

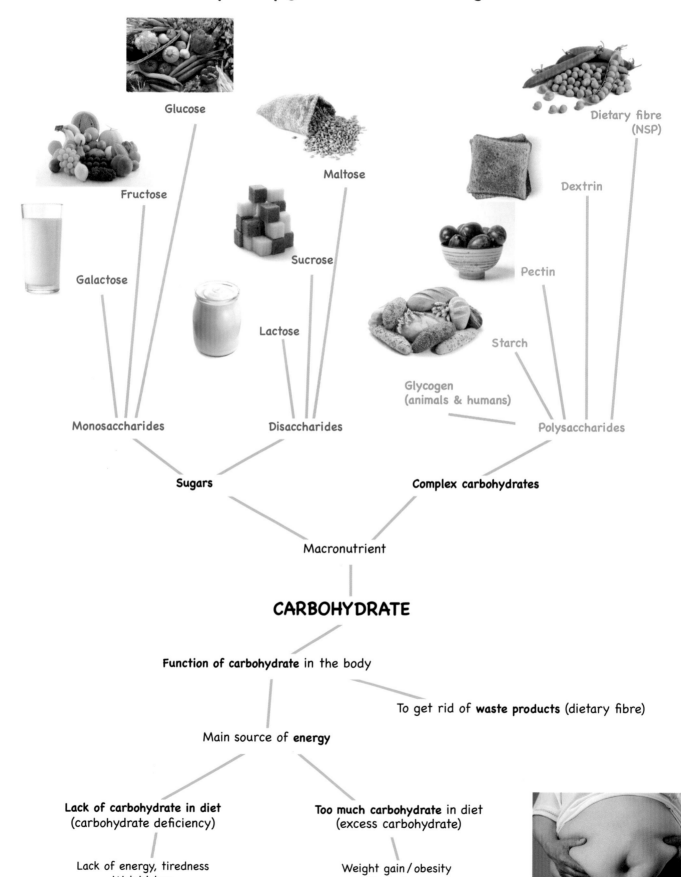

Glucose

Fructose

Maltose

Galactose

Sucrose

Lactose

Dietary fibre
(NSP)

Dextrin

Pectin

Starch

Glycogen
(animals & humans)

Monosaccharides

Disaccharides

Polysaccharides

Sugars

Complex carbohydrates

Macronutrient

CARBOHYDRATE

Function of carbohydrate in the body

To get rid of **waste products** (dietary fibre)

Main source of **energy**

Lack of carbohydrate in diet
(carbohydrate deficiency)

Lack of energy, tiredness
Weight loss
Severe weakness
Not enough fibre – constipation

Too much carbohydrate in diet
(excess carbohydrate)

Weight gain / obesity
Tooth decay
Type 2 diabetes

Activity 1.4

Look at the chart below and work out which carbohydrate each set of pictures is about. Explain how you worked out the answers from the picture clues:

Picture clues	Which carbohydrate is it?	Explain how you worked it out

Vitamins

Book-link:
1.1.4 Vitamins, pages 22–30

Key learning: What you must know about VITAMINS (micronutrients)

What you must know about vitamins	What vitamins do in the body (their functions)	Main sources of vitamins	Deficiency (not enough) of vitamins in the diet
Vitamin A (Retinol) Fat soluble	• Healthy skin • To see in dim light • Growth of children • Moist and healthy mucus membranes • Antioxidant (helps prevent heart disease and cancers)	**Animal foods (retinol):** milk; cheese; butter; eggs; liver, kidney; oily fish, vegetable fat spreads (added by law) **Plant foods (beta carotene):** cabbage, spinach, kale, lettuce; peas; orange/yellow/red vegetables and fruits (e.g. carrots, apricots, mango, papaya, peppers, tomatoes)	• Dry and infected skin and mucus membranes • Night blindness leading to total blindness • Poor growth in children • Poisonous if too much taken, e.g. in supplements, especially to unborn babies
Vitamin D (Cholecalciferol) Fat soluble	• Helps the body absorb calcium • Helps calcium to be laid down in bones and teeth for strength	Sunlight on skin; oily fish, meat, eggs, butter, vegetable fat spreads (added by law), fortified breakfast cereals	• Bones weaken and bend (rickets in children / osteomalacia in adults)
Vitamin E (Tocopherol) Fat soluble	• Antioxidant (helps prevent heart disease and cancers)	Soya, corn oil, olive oil, nuts, seeds, whole wheat, vegetable fat spreads	• Rare
Vitamin K (Phylloquinone) Fat soluble	• Helps blood clot after injury	Green, leafy vegetables, liver, cheese, green tea	• Rare but may happen in new born babies
Vitamin B1 (Thiamine) Water soluble	• Allows energy to be released from carbohydrates	Meat, especially pork, milk, cheese, eggs, vegetables, fresh and dried fruit, wholemeal bread, fortified breakfast cereals, flour	• Beri-beri – affects nerves and muscles
Vitamin B2 (Riboflavin) Water soluble	• Allows energy to be released from carbohydrates, fats and proteins	Milk and milk products, eggs, fortified breakfast rice, mushrooms	• Rare – sore corners of mouth
Vitamin B3 (Niacin) Water soluble	• Allows energy to be released from carbohydrates, fats and proteins	Beef, pork, wheat flour, maize flour, eggs, milk	• Pellagra – diarrhoea, dementia, dermatitis
Vitamin B9 (Folate) Water soluble	• Makes healthy red blood cells • Helps prevent spinal cord defects in unborn babies	Green leafy vegetables, yeast extract (e.g. Marmite); peas, chickpeas, asparagus; wholegrain rice; fruits; added to some breads and breakfast cereals	• Megaloblastic anaemia • Possibly spina bifida in new born babies
Vitamin B12 (Cobalamin) Water soluble	• Makes healthy red blood cells • Makes healthy nerve cells	Liver, meat, fish, cheese, fortified breakfast cereals, yeast	• Pernicious anaemia
Vitamin C (Ascorbic acid) Water soluble	• Helps the body absorb iron • Maintains connective tissue to bind body cells together • Antioxidant (helps prevent heart disease and cancers)	Fruits and vegetables, especially citrus fruits (e.g. oranges, lemons, limes and grapefruit), blackcurrants, kiwifruit, guavas, Brussels sprouts, cabbage, broccoli, new potatoes, milk and liver	• Scurvy • Anaemia (not enough iron absorbed) • Bleeding under skin • Loose teeth • Wounds do not heal

Key learning: What you must know about conserving certain vitamins when preparing and cooking food

Vitamin	How it is damaged or lost in food preparation and cooking
B1 (thiamine) B2 (riboflavin)	• Damaged by heat • Dissolves in water
B2 (riboflavin)	• Damaged by exposure to light
Vitamin C	• Damaged by heat • Dissolves in water • Damaged by exposure to air (oxygen)

How to prevent damage and loss of vitamins to vegetables and fruit		
During storage	• Store away from heat and light • Store in air-tight containers in a cool place • Store for as little time as possible	
During preparation	• Cut, grate, squeeze, chop just before cooking and serving • Avoid buying damaged and bruised fruits and vegetables	
During cooking	• Use only a little water for cooking • Boil water first then add foods • Cook (simmer) for minimum time until just tender • Serve straight away – avoid keeping them hot • Save the cooking water and use in gravy / soup • Steaming/microwaving instead of boiling vegetables saves more vitamins	

Revision tip

When answering a question about vitamins, make sure you show your knowledge and understanding of how some of them work with other nutrients in the body, e.g.:

Vitamin C helps the body absorb the mineral iron

Vitamin D helps the body absorb the mineral calcium

Vitamins B1, B2 and B3 help the body release energy from carbohydrates, fats and protein

Vitamin B9 works with vitamin B12 to make healthy red blood cells

Key terms you should try to use in your answers

Fat soluble: vitamins that are found in foods containing fats

Water soluble: vitamins that are found in foods with a high water content

THEORY INTO PRACTICE
– try this practical challenge

Plan and make a two-course main meal for two people that includes:

• A vegetable soup
• Some green, leafy vegetables and/or peas

Carry out a nutritional analysis of your chosen meal.

QUESTIONS

Using the results of the nutritional analysis and your knowledge of the effects of cooking on different vitamins, answer these questions:

• Explain which vitamins are provided in your chosen meal and which of these are likely to be damaged during cooking. *(3 marks)*

• Explain how you would minimise the amount of damage to the vitamins when you prepare, cook and serve them. *(3 marks)*

Activity 1.5

Look at the chart below and work out which vitamin each set of pictures is about. Explain how you worked out the answers from the picture clues:

Picture clues	Which vitamin is it?	Explain how you worked it out

5 Minerals

Book-link:
1.1.5 Minerals, pages 30–35

Key learning: What you must know about MINERALS (micronutrients)

Mineral	What minerals do in the body (their functions)	Main sources of minerals	Deficiency (not enough) of minerals in diet
Calcium	• Strong **bones and teeth** • Makes **nerves and muscles** work • Helps **blood clot** after injury	Milk, cheese, yogurt; green leafy vegetables; canned fish; enriched soya drinks; wheat flour (added by law to plain white flour)	• Bones and teeth weaken • Bones bend • Nerves and muscles don't work properly • Blood will not clot after injury
Iron	• Makes **haemoglobin** in **red blood cells** to carry **oxygen** to all body cells to produce **energy**	Red meat, kidney, liver; wholemeal bread, added to wheat flour (except wholemeal); green leafy vegetables (e.g. watercress, spinach, cabbage); egg yolk; dried apricots; lentils; cocoa, plain chocolate; curry powder; fortified breakfast cereals	• Iron deficiency anaemia • Tiredness and lack of energy • Weakness • Pale skin complexion • Weak and spilt nails • **Too much iron:** poisonous if too much taken, e.g. in supplements
Sodium	• Controls **water** in body • Makes **nerves and muscles** work properly	Salt (**sodium** chloride); salted foods; cheese, yeast extract, stock cubes, gravies and seasonings, snack foods (e.g. crisps), canned fish, bacon, ham, dried fish, soy sauce, salted butter, fast foods and many ready meals; baking powder (cakes, biscuits, baked desserts); takeaway foods	• Muscle cramps • **Too much sodium (salt):** leads to high blood pressure and cardio–vascular disease
Fluoride	• Strengthens **tooth enamel** and bones	Seafood, fish, tea, some water supplies	• Weak enamel – more chance of tooth decay • **Too much fluoride:** may lead to discoloured teeth
Iodine	• Makes **thyroxin** in thyroid gland to control **metabolic rate** of body	Seafood, vegetables, dairy foods	• Swelling in neck (goitre)
Phosphorus	• Strong **bones and teeth** • **Energy** release • Makes **cell membranes** especially in the brain	Wide range of foods	• Rare

Revision tip

When answering a question about minerals, make sure you are clear about the health conditions and diseases that are linked to them, for example:

Calcium has four health conditions and diseases linked to it:

Rickets – caused by a deficiency (not enough) of vitamin D in children, which means that calcium can't be absorbed and put into the bones.

Osteomalacia – this is the adult form of rickets.

Peak bone mass – the age at which the bones should contain the maximum amount of minerals and are at their strongest and most dense (30–35 years old).

Osteoporosis – after peak bone mass is reached, the bones naturally start to lose minerals and gradually weaken. The minerals are not replaced. The bones gradually weaken and in some people can become very fragile and break easily.

vitamins & minerals

Applying your learning

• Plan a two-course main meal for a teenage girl who is suffering from anaemia. Explain how your meal will provide the right nutrients to help to cure the anaemia.

Activity 1.6

Look at the chart below and work out which mineral each set of pictures is about. Explain how you worked out the answers from the picture clues:

Picture clues	Which mineral is it?	Explain how you worked it out

6 Water

Book-link:
1.1.6 Water, pages 36–37

Key learning: What you must know about WATER

What you must know about water

In your answers, you need to know how to explain:

Further information you can add to extend your answers:

What water does in the body (its functions)	• Controls body temperature • Needed for chemical reactions in body • Removes waste products from body • Keeps mucous membranes moist and healthy • Keeps skin moist and healthy • Needed for all body fluids • Found in all body cells	• Heat is removed from the body by sweating • Waste products leave the body in urine (made in the kidneys) and faeces (made in the large intestine) • Water controls the concentration of substances (e.g. sodium) in the blood
Main sources of water in the diet	• Drinking water (tap water) • Naturally found in many foods – milk, milk products, fruit, vegetables, meat, fish, eggs • Added to many foods – soup, sauces, pastries, breads, boiled rice, pasta, beans, pulses, etc.	• Tap water is good quality and safe to drink in the UK and much cheaper than bottled water • Discarded plastic water bottles have a major impact on environmental sustainability and pollution
What happens if you do not have enough water (dehydration)	• You become thirsty • A headache often starts • **Dehydration** – the urine becomes very dark in colour • You feel weak and sick • The body overheats • You become confused • The blood pressure and heart rate change	• Headaches may be caused because the blood has become too concentrated • The colour of urine is a good indicator of dehydration:

1	Good
2	Good
3	Fair
4	Dehydrated
5	Dehydrated
6	Very dehydrated
7	Severe dehydration

• Chemical reactions in the body may be affected
• If the body rises above 37°C, this is dangerous
• The brain becomes affected by lack of water
• The volume of the blood decreases which affects the blood pressure and heart rate

What happens if you have too much water	• Substances in the blood become over-diluted • Vital organs in the body start to fail, e.g. heart, kidneys • May cause death	• It is a rare cause of death, but it has happened to some people who have done a lot of exercise then had a lot of water to drink in one go
What is the recommended amount of water per day	• In the UK: 1–2 litres of water or other fluids a day (6–8 average glasses)	• More water will be needed in hotter climates and when doing a lot of physical activity

Key terms you should try to use in your answers

Hydrated: the body has enough water

Dehydrated: the body does not have enough water

Multiple choice challenge

Have a go at answering these questions. They are worth **one mark** each. Answers are on page 145.

1. **Protein is needed for:**
   - a) Growth
   - b) Repair
   - c) Maintenance of the body
   - d) All of these

2. **How many amino acids are essential for children?**
   - a) 5
   - b) 10
   - c) 9
   - d) 7

3. **Low biological value proteins:**
   - a) Contain all the essential amino acids
   - b) Contain no essential amino acids
   - c) Are missing one or more essential amino acids
   - d) Are missing one or more essential fatty acids

4. **High biological value proteins are found in:**
   - a) Meat, fish, eggs, milk, cheese, soya beans
   - b) Cereals, pulses, nuts, seeds, tofu
   - c) Meat, fish, eggs, milk, gelatine, nuts
   - d) Tofu, tempeh, texture vegetable protein, wheat

5. **Saturated fatty acids are found mainly in:**
   - a) Lard, ghee, olive oil, butter
   - b) Butter, avocados, olive oil, coconut oil
   - c) Lard, ghee, palm oil, butter
   - d) Lard, ghee, olive oil, suet

6. **Visible fats are found in:**
   - a) Fried foods, chocolate, cakes, biscuits
   - b) Lard, butter, suet, meat
   - c) Vegetable fat spread, meat, puff pastry, potato chips
   - d) Lard, butter, cakes, meat

7. **Fat is stored in the body in:**
   - a) Blood cells
   - b) Cartilage
   - c) Adipose tissue
   - d) Muscle tissue

8. **Fatty / oily foods provide the body with:**
   - a) Vitamin B group
   - b) Vitamin C
   - c) Vitamins A, D, E, K
   - d) Calcium

9. **Fatty foods are known as:**
   - a) Low energy foods
   - b) Energy light foods
   - c) Energy dense foods
   - d) Energy 'Lite' foods

10. **Eating too much fat can lead to:**
    - a) Osteoporosis
    - b) Coronary heart disease
    - c) Night blindness
    - d) Scurvy

11. **The following are all types of sugar:**
    - a) Glucose, galactose, fructose
    - b) Glycerine, gluten, collagen
    - c) Lipids, insulin, glycol
    - d) Glucose, maltose, glycerol

12. **The following are all monosaccharides:**
    - a) Lactose, glucose, galactose
    - b) Glucose, galactose, fructose
    - c) Fructose, maltose, glucose
    - d) Glucose, starch, fructose

13. **The following are all complex carbohydrates (polysaccharides):**
    - a) Glucose, maltose, starch
    - b) Glucose, fructose, pectin
    - c) Glycerol, glycogen, glucose
    - d) Dietary fibre, starch, pectin

14. **Another name for NSP (non-starch polysaccharide) is:**
    - a) Dietary fibre
    - b) Cholesterol
    - c) Glycogen
    - d) Lipid

15. **Thiamine is used in the body to:**
    - a) Strengthen the skeleton
    - b) See in the dark
    - c) Release energy from carbohydrates
    - d) Help the body to absorb iron

16. **A deficiency of thiamine results in:**
    - a) Pellagra
    - b) Beri-beri
    - c) Anaemia
    - d) Influenza

17. **A deficiency of niacin results in:**
    - a) Pellagra
    - b) Beri-beri
    - c) Anaemia
    - d) Influenza

18. **Vitamin B9 (folate) helps to prevent:**
    - a) Scurvy
    - b) Osteoporosis
    - c) Spina bifida
    - d) Beri-beri

19. **Ascorbic acid (vitamin C) is needed by the body to:**
    - a) Absorb iron, maintain connective tissue, be an antioxidant
    - b) Absorb iron, produce white blood cells, be an antioxidant
    - c) Absorb iron, produce digestive juices, be an antioxidant
    - d) Absorb calcium, maintain connective tissue, produce red blood cells

20. **A deficiency of vitamin C leads to:**
    - a) Anaemia
    - b) Leaking blood vessels
    - c) Scurvy
    - d) All of these

21. **These vitamins are all antioxidants:**
- [ ] a) A, B, C
- [ ] b) A, D, B
- [ ] c) A, C, E
- [ ] d) A, E, B

22. **In animal foods, vitamin A is known as:**
- [ ] a) Retina
- [ ] b) Retinol
- [ ] c) Visual purple
- [ ] d) Beta carotene

23. **A deficiency of vitamin A causes:**
- [ ] a) Poor growth, infections, night blindness
- [ ] b) Poor growth, infections, spina bifida
- [ ] c) Poor growth, hallucinations, night blindness
- [ ] d) Leaking blood vessels, poor growth, blindness

24. **Vitamin D helps the body absorb:**
- [ ] a) Calcium
- [ ] b) Iodine
- [ ] c) Fluoride
- [ ] d) Iron

25. **A deficiency of calcium leads to:**
- [ ] a) Weak bones, low peak bone mass, low blood pressure
- [ ] b) Weak bones, low blood pressure, blood will not clot properly
- [ ] c) Weak bones, low peak bone mass, blood will not clot properly
- [ ] d) Muscle cramps, blood will not clot properly, low blood pressure

26. **Lack of iron leads to:**
- [ ] a) Toothache
- [ ] b) Anaemia
- [ ] c) Weak bones
- [ ] d) Blindness

27. **Too much salt in the diet can lead to:**
- [ ] a) Low blood pressure
- [ ] b) Anaemia
- [ ] c) High blood pressure
- [ ] d) Weak eyesight

28. **Iodine is needed to produce:**
- [ ] a) Growth hormones
- [ ] b) Thyroid hormones
- [ ] c) Adrenalin
- [ ] d) Digestive enzymes

29. **Fluoride is needed to:**
- [ ] a) Strengthen tooth enamel
- [ ] b) Strengthen muscles
- [ ] c) Strengthen nerve cells
- [ ] d) Strengthen the gums

30. **Water helps the body to get rid of:**
- [ ] a) Heat
- [ ] b) Urine
- [ ] c) Faeces
- [ ] d) All of these

Knowledge check – can you recall...?

(Answers on page 146)

1. What protein complementation means? *(1 mark)*
2. What amino acids are? *(1 mark)*
3. The functions of protein in the body? *(3 marks)*
4. Five foods that contain HBV proteins? *(5 marks)*
5. Five foods that contain LBV proteins? *(5 marks)*
6. Three things that happen to people if they don't have enough protein? *(3 marks)*
7. What the name of a fat molecule is? *(1 mark)*
8. The functions of fat in the body? *(4 marks)*
9. What a fatty acid is? *(1 mark)*
10. Four foods that contain mainly saturated fatty acids? *(4 marks)*
11. Four foods that contain mainly unsaturated fatty acids? *(4 marks)*
12. Why fatty foods are energy dense? *(1 mark)*
13. Why cakes, pastries, biscuits, crisps, etc., contain invisible fat? *(1 mark)*
14. Two health conditions that people might get if they eat too much fat? *(2 marks)*
15. The functions of carbohydrate in the body? *(2 marks)*
16. The two main groups of carbohydrates? *(2 marks)*
17. The names of the three monosaccharides? *(3 marks)*
18. The names of the three disaccharides? *(3 marks)*
19. The names of the four polysaccharides found in foods? *(4 marks)*
20. The name of the polysaccharide made by animals and humans in their bodies? *(1 mark)*
21. Two health conditions that people might get if they eat too much carbohydrate? *(2 marks)*
22. What free sugars are and why they should be limited in the diet? *(2 marks)*
23. Which vitamins are fat soluble? *(4 marks)*
24. Which vitamins help energy to be released from food in the body? *(3 marks)*
25. Which vitamin helps the body absorb iron? *(1 mark)*
26. Which vitamin helps the body absorb calcium? *(1 mark)*
27. Which three vitamins are antioxidants? *(3 marks)*
28. Which vitamin is made in the body from the action of sunlight on the skin? *(1 mark)*
29. Which two vitamins help the body to make healthy red blood cells? *(2 marks)*
30. Which mineral causes high blood pressure if you have too much of it in food? *(1 mark)*
31. The name of the deficiency disease caused by not enough vitamin C? *(1 mark)*
32. The name of the deficiency disease in children caused by not enough vitamin D? *(1 mark)*

33. The name of the deficiency disease in adults caused by not enough vitamin D? *(1 mark)*
34. The name of the deficiency disease caused by not enough vitamin A? *(1 mark)*
35. The name of the deficiency disease caused by not enough vitamin B1? *(1 mark)*
36. The name of the deficiency disease caused by not enough vitamin B12? *(1 mark)*
37. The function of vitamin K in the body? *(1 mark)*
38. The name of the deficiency disease caused by not enough iron? *(1 mark)*
39. Five reasons why the body needs water? *(5 marks)*
40. Three symptoms of being dehydrated? *(3 marks)*

Stretch and challenge questions

1. In the UK, Public Health England have recommended that the price of high-sugar products, such as soft drinks, should be increased by adding a sugar tax to them.

   (Ref: Public Health England, October 2015: *Sugar Reduction – The evidence for action* www.gov.uk/government/uploads/system/uploads/attachment_data/file/470179/Sugar_reduction_The_evidence_for_action.pdf)

   Analyse why this recommendation has been made, and explain what it is hoped will be achieved by the introduction of the sugar tax. *(8 marks)*

2. In major sporting competitions such as the Olympic Games and World Athletics Championships, dietitians and nutritionists are involved to ensure that team members follow a dietary programme suited to their particular needs during training and events.

   a) Analyse and explain the nutritional needs of track athletes who run in events such as the 100m and 200m sprint, hurdles, 4 × 100m relay, and 5,000 and 10,000 metres races. *(5 marks)*

   b) Plan a two-course lunch for a track athlete and evaluate how it would help them to maintain their fitness. *(4 marks)*

   c) Explain why hydration is particularly important for these athletes. *(3 marks)*

3. Analyse and explain the reasons for the following practices in food preparation and cooking, giving examples in your answers:

   a) Choosing and buying vegetables and fruits that are as fresh as possible and not damaged or bruised. *(2 marks)*

   b) Peeling, chopping, grating and slicing vegetables and fruits as close as possible to the time that they are cooked or served. *(2 marks)*

   c) Boiling green vegetables in the minimum amount of water for the minimum amount of time. *(2 marks)*

   d) Steaming green vegetables instead of boiling them. *(2 marks)*

Chapter 2: Nutritional needs and health

Book-link:
1.2.1 Making informed food choices for a varied and balanced diet, pages 38–57

1 Nutritional needs

What do you need to know?

You now know about the **nutrients** in food.

Next you need to know:

- What a **healthy balanced diet** is
- How different foods give us a healthy balanced **diet**
- How to provide a healthy balanced diet for people at different **life stages**
- How to provide a healthy balanced diet for people with different **dietary needs**
- How to analyse and interpret nutritional information

Key learning: DIETARY GUIDELINES

What you must know about dietary guidelines

In your answers, you need to know how to explain:

Further information you can add to extend your answers:

What the Eatwell Guide is and who it is for

What the Eatwell Guide means:

- It is based on the five food groups
- The segments match the government's recommendations for a diet that would provide all the nutrients needed by a healthy adult or child (over the age of 5 years)
- From 2 to 5 years, children should gradually start eating a greater variety of foods as shown in the Eatwell Guide

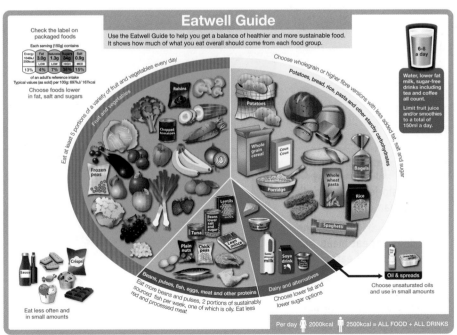

What a healthy, balanced diet means

What 'diet' means:

- **Diet**: means the food that you eat every day
- Don't confuse the word 'diet' with trying to lose weight by reducing calories
- **Healthy, balanced diet** contains the **correct** amounts of carbohydrates, fats, proteins, vitamins, minerals and water that people, at different life stages, need for good health, to grow properly, be active and maintain a healthy body

There are also special diets:

- Low-fat
- Calorie controlled
- Low salt
- Low sugar
- High fibre
- Gluten-free
- Lactose-free
- Energy dense
- Lacto-vegetarian
- Lacto-ovo vegetarian
- Vegan

What the dietary guidelines are

There are eight guidelines

1. Base your meals on starchy foods

2. Eat lots of fruit and vegetables

3. Eat more fish – including a portion of oily fish each week

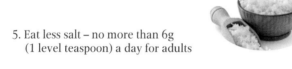

4. Cut down on saturated fat and sugar

5. Eat less salt – no more than 6g (1 level teaspoon) a day for adults

6. Get active and be a healthy weight

7. Don't get thirsty – drink plenty of water

8. Don't skip breakfast

Dietary guidelines are designed to:

- Advise people about how to choose a variety of foods to get a healthy balanced diet
- Encourage people to stay active to be fit and well
- Help people understand the importance of being a healthy weight
- Advise people to drink plenty of water so they don't get thirsty and dehydrated
- Recommend that people eat regular meals to keep them healthy

---

Key terms you should try to use in your answers

Healthy, balanced diet: a **diet** that contains the **correct** proportions of carbohydrates, fats, proteins, vitamins, minerals and water necessary for good health, to grow properly, be active and maintain a healthy body

Diet: the food that you eat every day. There are also special diets (e.g. a low-fat diet, a calorie controlled diet, a vegetarian diet)

Lacto-vegetarian: someone who does not eat meat, fish or eggs, but will eat milk and milk products

Lacto-ovo-vegetarian: someone who does not eat meat or fish but will eat milk, milk products and eggs

Revision tip

Remember that the Eatwell Guide is for an overall healthy diet. It does not mean that every meal eaten every day should contain all the different food groups.

Activity 2.1

Using your knowledge of the nutrients in foods, match up the dietary guidelines with the correct reason why each is recommended:

Dietary guideline

Why it is recommended

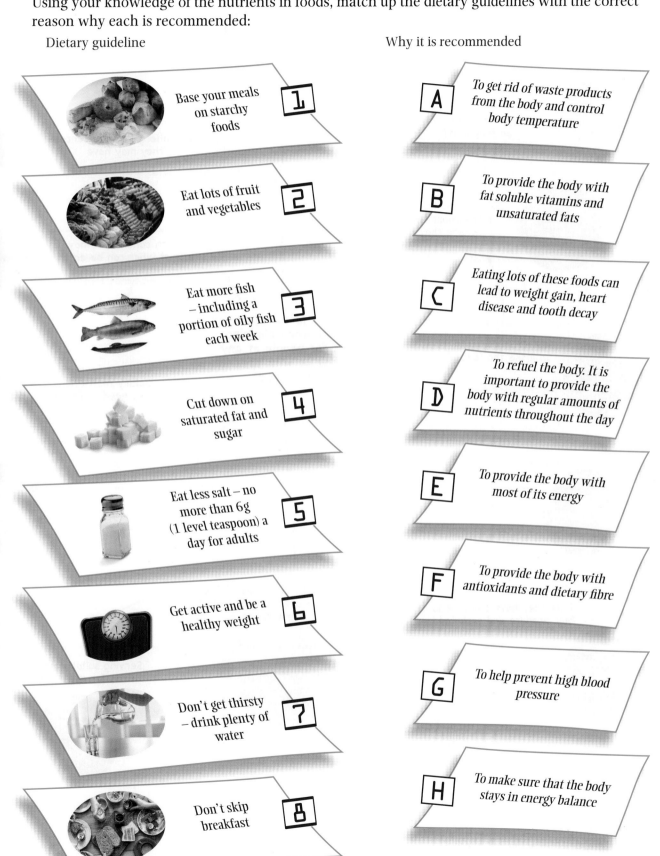

1 Base your meals on starchy foods

2 Eat lots of fruit and vegetables

3 Eat more fish – including a portion of oily fish each week

4 Cut down on saturated fat and sugar

5 Eat less salt – no more than 6g (1 level teaspoon) a day for adults

6 Get active and be a healthy weight

7 Don't get thirsty – drink plenty of water

8 Don't skip breakfast

A To get rid of waste products from the body and control body temperature

B To provide the body with fat soluble vitamins and unsaturated fats

C Eating lots of these foods can lead to weight gain, heart disease and tooth decay

D To refuel the body. It is important to provide the body with regular amounts of nutrients throughout the day

E To provide the body with most of its energy

F To provide the body with antioxidants and dietary fibre

G To help prevent high blood pressure

H To make sure that the body stays in energy balance

Key learning: General rules for planning meals

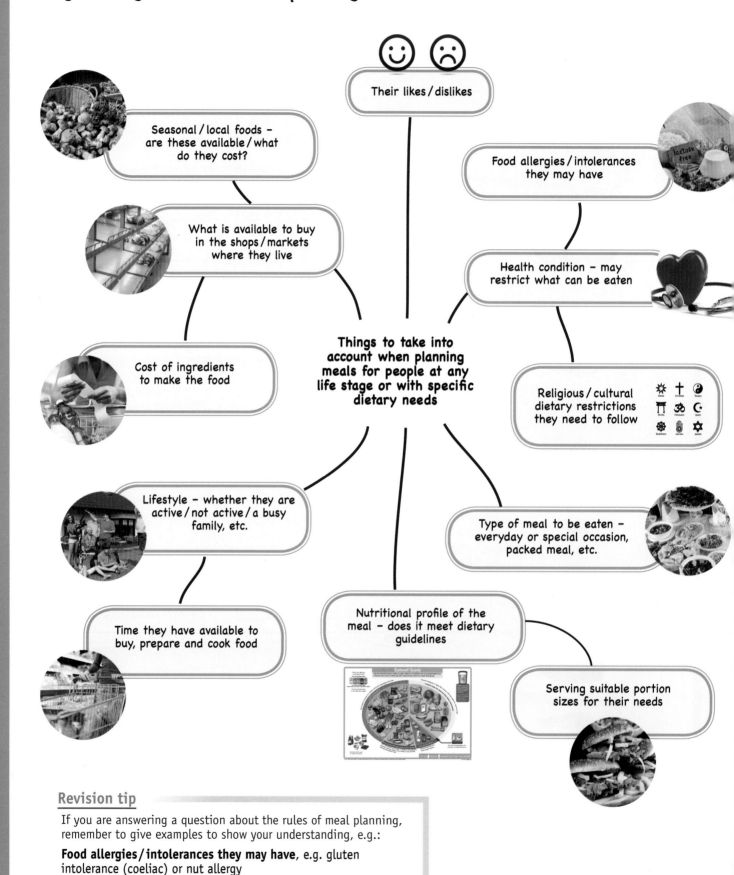

Their likes / dislikes

Seasonal / local foods – are these available / what do they cost?

Food allergies / intolerances they may have

What is available to buy in the shops / markets where they live

Health condition – may restrict what can be eaten

Cost of ingredients to make the food

Things to take into account when planning meals for people at any life stage or with specific dietary needs

Religious / cultural dietary restrictions they need to follow

Lifestyle – whether they are active / not active / a busy family, etc.

Type of meal to be eaten – everyday or special occasion, packed meal, etc.

Time they have available to buy, prepare and cook food

Nutritional profile of the meal – does it meet dietary guidelines

Serving suitable portion sizes for their needs

Revision tip

If you are answering a question about the rules of meal planning, remember to give examples to show your understanding, e.g.:

Food allergies / intolerances they may have, e.g. gluten intolerance (coeliac) or nut allergy

Cost of food, e.g. buying supermarket value brands for foods such as cheese, canned tomatoes and pasta, etc., can save money

Key learning: Planning balanced meals for different life stages

What you must know about planning balanced meals

In your answers, you need to know how to explain:

Further information you can add to extend your answers:

Points that apply to pre-school children 1–4 years

The best eating habits and lifestyle choices for this life stage:

- Regular meals and drinks
- Serve small portions
- Try new foods regularly
- Eat fresh and raw foods as well as cooked ones
- Allow them to eat until they feel full – do not expect them to finish everything
- Be aware of choking hazards with foods

Encourage:

- Drinking water and whole milk
- Share and enjoy food as a group
- Happy meal times – sitting at a table if possible
- Involving children in choosing and buying food
- Encourage tooth care – cleaning regularly and not eating too many sugary foods

- Body growth and development is rapid
- Energy needs are high
- All nutrients are important especially protein, vitamins and minerals
- Eatwell Guide does not fully apply but gradually move towards it
- Limit the amount of free sugars and salt eaten

Discourage:

- Eating snacks between meals

Points that apply to children 5–12 years

The best eating habits and lifestyle choices for this life stage:

- Regular meals and drinks – especially breakfast
- Follow the Eatwell Guide
- Continue to try new foods regularly
- Eat fresh and raw foods as well as cooked ones
- Share and enjoy food as a group / family

Encourage:

- Children to find out about food
- Children to drink water
- Children to go shopping for food and help preparing family meals

- Body growth and development is rapid
- Energy needs are high – children should be physically active
- All nutrients are important especially protein, vitamins and minerals
- Limit the amount of free sugars and salt eaten

Discourage:

- Long use of computers / phones / TV to avoid them becoming overweight due to being inactive
- Drinking sugary fizzy drinks
- Eating snacks between meals
- Eating too many ready-prepared meals and fast food

Points that apply to adolescents (teenagers)

The best eating habits and lifestyle choices for this life stage:

- Regular meals and drinks – always eat breakfast
- Drink plenty of water
- Continue to try new foods regularly
- Follow the Eatwell Guide
- Eat fresh and raw foods as well as cooked ones
- Take regular exercise to stay fit and maintain a healthy weight
- Spend regular time outside in the sun to make vitamin D in the body

Encourage:

- Teenagers to find out about food
- Teenagers to be involved in cooking meals in the home
- Teenagers to go shopping for food and help plan family meals
- Teenagers to get plenty of sleep

All nutrients are important especially:

- **Calcium/vitamin D** – so skeleton strengthens and reaches peak bone mass when they are adults
- **Iron and vitamin C:** (especially girls) to avoid anaemia
- **B group vitamins:** to help the body use energy and the brain to concentrate
- **Fibre:** to maintain a healthy digestive system

Discourage:

- Eating too many energy-dense foods / meals
- Eating lots of sugar and salt
- Drinking sugary fizzy drinks which may affect how the bones take up minerals
- Eating too many ready-prepared meals and fast food

Points that apply to adults	The best eating habits and lifestyle choices for this life stage:	• Metabolic rate slows down, so weight gain may happen if energy balance is wrong

The best eating habits and lifestyle choices for this life stage:

- Regular meals and drinks – always eat breakfast
- Drink plenty of water
- Follow the Eatwell Guide
- Take regular, load-bearing (e.g. running, jumping, walking) exercise to stay fit and maintain a healthy weight
- Spend regular time outside in the sun to make vitamin D in the body
- Get plenty of sleep
- Try to avoid too much stress

- Metabolic rate slows down, so weight gain may happen if energy balance is wrong
- All nutrients are important especially:
- **Calcium/vitamin D** – skeleton reaches peak bone mass around 30 years of age and gradually starts to lose minerals and become weakened after this age
- **Iron and vitamin C:** (especially women) to avoid anaemia
- **B group vitamins:** to help the body use energy and the brain to concentrate
- **Fibre:** to maintain a healthy digestive system

Avoid:

- Eating too many energy-dense foods/meals
- Eating lots of sugar and salt
- Eating and drinking foods with a lot of sugar, fat and salt

---

Points that apply to elderly adults

The best eating habits and lifestyle choices for this life stage:

- Eat regular well-balanced meals and drinks – always eat breakfast
- Eat smaller portions as the appetite will decrease and metabolic rate will slow down
- Some nutrients will not be so well absorbed in the body, so eat plenty of fruit and vegetables and iron-rich foods
- Eat plenty of fibre to maintain a healthy digestive system
- Drink plenty of water
- Follow the Eatwell Guide
- Take regular exercise to stay fit and maintain a healthy weight
- Spend regular time outside in the sun to make vitamin D in the body

- Metabolic rate slows down, so weight gain may happen if energy balance is wrong
- All nutrients are important especially:
- **Calcium/vitamin D** – skeleton gradually starts to lose minerals and become weakened, which becomes worse in women after the menopause. Can develop into osteoporosis in men and women.
- **Iron and vitamin C:** (especially women) to avoid anaemia
- **B group vitamins:** to help the body use energy and to help prevent memory loss
- **Fibre:** to maintain a healthy digestive system
- **Vitamins A,C and E:** to help prevent age-related eye conditions. Discourage eating lots of sugar and salt

Avoid:

- Eating too many energy-dense foods/meals (unless advised by a doctor or dietitian)
- Eating and drinking foods with a lot of sugar, fat and salt

---

Key terms you should try to use in your answers

Life stages: phases of development that people go through during their life, such as infancy (babyhood), childhood, adolescence (teenagers), adulthood and the elderly

Revision tip

The information in the table is related to planning meals for different life stages.

Extended examination questions can ask about what to consider when meal planning for a different life stage, e.g. teenagers.

It is important to always plan your answer before starting to write. This will allow you to include all the key information. Using bullet points/listing key words is a good technique before starting to answer the question.

Key learning: Planning balanced meals for specific groups

What they do eat ✓		What they do not eat ✗

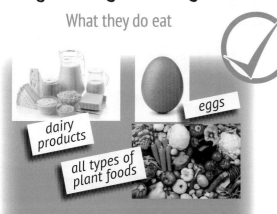

dairy products

eggs

all types of plant foods

Lacto-ovo-vegetarian diet

meat

fish

shellfish

gelatine

dairy products

all types of plant foods

Lacto-vegetarian diet

meat

fish

gelatine

shellfish

eggs

all plant foods

protein alternatives: tofu, tempeh, TVP

Vegan diet

all animal foods

fish and shellfish

dairy products

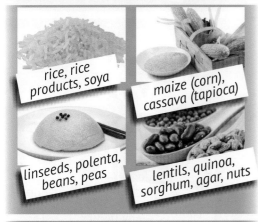

rice, rice products, soya

maize (corn), cassava (tapioca)

linseeds, polenta, beans, peas

lentils, quinoa, sorghum, agar, nuts

Coeliac diet

wheat and wheat products

bread, cakes

barley, oats, rye products

biscuits, pastries

Lactose intolerance diet

specially produced lactose-free dairy foods

milk, milk products, and any food containing milk products

What they do eat

What they do not eat

fruits, vegetables

wholegrains

rice, peas

beans, lentils

High fibre diet

white flour and products

white rice

smooth fruit juice

. . . .

fresh fruits and vegetables

milk, unsweetened milk products

Low sugar diet

free sugars that have been added to cakes, biscuits, drinks, confectionery, desserts, sauces, ice cream, breakfast cereals, honey, syrup, jam, etc.

. . . .

naturally low-fat foods, e.g. fruits vegetables, cereals, white fish, fat reduced cheese, spreads, milk, etc.

Fat reduced diet

full-fat dairy foods, pastries, meats, crisps, chips, doughnuts, cakes, biscuits, fried foods, desserts, ice cream

. . . .

fruits, vegetables, milk, eggs

Low salt (sodium) diet

yeast extract, cheese, dried fish, canned fish, soy sauce, ketchup, pickles, many ready meals and takeaways, snack foods, cakes, biscuits, scones

Applying your learning

An 18-year-old female has decided to follow a vegan diet.

Explain why it is important that she receives enough of the following nutrients:

- Protein
- Iron
- Calcium

Plan a day's meals for her which include good sources of protein, iron and calcium.

THEORY INTO PRACTICE
– try this practical challenge

Plan and make a tasty and balanced two-course evening meal for two teenagers, which can be prepared, cooked and served in 30 minutes. Carry out a nutritional analysis of the meal.

QUESTIONS

Using your knowledge of nutrients and dietary guidelines, answer these questions:

- Using your nutritional analysis to help you, explain how the meal you have planned meets the dietary guidelines for teenagers. *(3 marks)*
- Explain what time-saving methods you have used to prepare and cook the meal within the time allowed. *(3 marks)*

2 Energy needs

Book-link:
1.2.2 Energy needs, pages 58–62

What do you need to know?

You now know about the **dietary guidelines** for a **healthy balanced diet**.

Next you need to know:

- The importance of energy in the diet
- How we get energy from food
- Why the body needs energy
- Why energy balance is important

Key learning: Energy in the body and in the diet

What you must know about energy in the body

In your answers, you need to know how to explain:

Further information you can add to extend your answers:

Functions of energy in the body	Energy is needed by the body for: • Growth • Movement • Body warmth • Production of sound • Brain function • Chemical reactions	• Energy is measured in either kilocalories (kcals) or kilojoules (kJ) • 1 kcal = 4.2 kJ

		Typical values
		Energy 1570kJ / 375kcal, 100g contains; 710kJ / 170kcal, 45g serving contains Protein 10.3g, 4.6g Carbohydrate 73.8g of which sugars Fat 15.0

Main sources of energy in the diet	• Carbohydrate • Fat • Protein   	• 1g pure **carbohydrate** = 3.75 kcal / 16kJ • 1g pure **fat** = 9 kcal / 37kJ • 1g pure **protein** = 4 kcal / 16kJ • Energy from excess carbohydrates converts into fat in the body • **Glucose** is the form in which energy is used in the body • Fats and oils have the same energy value • Fat is a store of energy in the body • Fat is converted into glucose in the body when there is not enough carbohydrate available • Protein is only used for energy if there is not enough carbohydrate or fat available • Foods containing a lot of fat and sugar are called **energy dense**

Effects of a deficiency of energy in the diet	• Body loses weight as fat stores are used up 	• Fat stores are gradually used up, so it takes time for weight loss to happen • This is the basis of weight reducing diets, which should be followed in a controlled way so that not too much weight is lost
Effects of an excess of energy in the diet	• Energy is stored as body fat • The weight of the body gradually increases • Obesity may be the result of continuous excess energy in the diet 	• Gradual weight gain 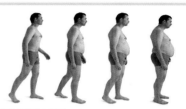
The amount of energy needed each day	**The recommended amount of energy from different nutrients each day is:** • **Carbohydrate:** 50% • **Fat:** 35% or less • **Protein:** 15%	• For carbohydrate, most energy should come from starch and intrinsic sugars (naturally found in foods, e,g, vegetables and milk) • No more than 5% should come from fruit sugars, e.g. fruit juice and free sugars (added to foods)
What affects the amount of energy needed by the body	**The amount of energy needed is influenced by:** • A person's **metabolic rate** • How **active** someone is To stay at a healthy weight, the body needs to be in energy balance: 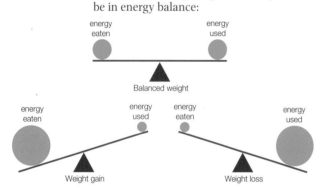	**Basal metabolic rate (BMR):** • Amount of energy needed to keep us alive and the body working normally • Varies according to age, gender, body size, physical activity level **Physical activity level (PAL):** • Physical activity reduces risk of developing a range of diet-related diseases, e.g. obesity and heart disease • Improves strength of skeleton and muscles • Keeps brain alert **Energy balance:** • The amount of energy consumed in food must be used up by the **BMR** and **PAL** • **Too much energy** consumed leads to **weight gain** • **Too little energy** consumed leads to **weight loss**

Key terms you should try to use in your answers

Energy dense: a food that contains a lot of fat and/or carbohydrate and has a high energy value

BMR: Basal metabolic rate is the amount of energy we need to keep our body alive

PAL: this means physical activity level, and is the amount of energy we use for movement and physical activity every day

Energy balance: the amount of energy we get from food each day is the same as the amount of energy we use each day

Applying your learning

Many school-aged children and teenagers in the UK have been identified as being overweight or obese.

• Give two reasons why the numbers of school-aged children and teenagers becoming overweight and obese have significantly increased in recent years.

• Describe two likely long-term effects on the health of these children and teenagers if they remain overweight or obese.

• Suggest three ways in which children and teenagers can avoid becoming overweight or obese, giving reasons and examples in your answers.

Here is a revision mind map to help you learn about energy:

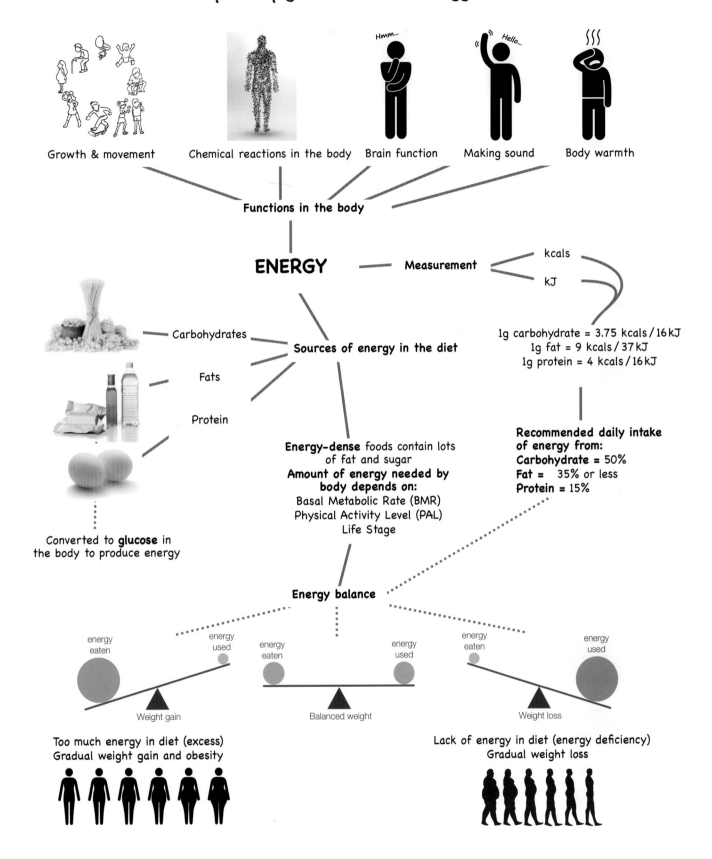

Growth & movement   Chemical reactions in the body   Brain function   Making sound   Body warmth

Functions in the body

ENERGY

Measurement

kcals

kJ

Carbohydrates

Fats

Protein

Sources of energy in the diet

1g carbohydrate = 3.75 kcals / 16 kJ
1g fat = 9 kcals / 37 kJ
1g protein = 4 kcals / 16 kJ

Converted to **glucose** in the body to produce energy

Energy-dense foods contain lots of fat and sugar
Amount of energy needed by body depends on:
Basal Metabolic Rate (BMR)
Physical Activity Level (PAL)
Life Stage

Recommended daily intake of energy from:
Carbohydrate = 50%
Fat = 35% or less
Protein = 15%

Energy balance

energy eaten   energy used
Weight gain

energy eaten   energy used
Balanced weight

energy eaten   energy used
Weight loss

Too much energy in diet (excess)
Gradual weight gain and obesity

Lack of energy in diet (energy deficiency)
Gradual weight loss

Activity 2.2

Look at the pictures in the chart below and identify which of the foods are <u>energy dense</u>.

For each one you identify, explain why the ingredients it contains make it energy dense.

For each one you do not identify, explain why it is <u>not</u> energy dense.

Food	Energy dense? or Not energy dense?	Explain why you have given this answer
cucumber and lettuce		
jam doughnut		
chocolate chip cookie		
low fat strawberry yogurt		
pork pie		
lentil and vegetable soup		
chips, cheese and mayonnaise		
kebab and fries		
sausage roll made with puff pastry		
fresh fruit salad		

3 How to carry out nutritional analysis

Book-link: 1.2.3
How to carry out nutritional analysis,
pages 63–69

Key learning: Nutrient profiles and carrying out nutritional analysis

Nutrient profile

- Most foods contain more than one nutrient
- Some foods contain many nutrients, e.g. milk
- Some foods contain very few nutrients, e.g. sugar
- Nutrient profiles for different foods are available in books and on nutritional analysis software computer programs
- Nutritional analysis means finding out how much of each nutrient is in a quantity of food (usually 100g or 100ml), or a whole recipe, or a food product you make, or buy

Activity 2.3

Compare, contrast and analyse the two nutrient profiles shown for milk and fizzy lemonade.

Comment on:

1. The differences and similarities between the two drinks
2. Explain, with reasons, why you think one is more suitable for children to drink than the other.

Nutrient profile: milk

MACRONUTRIENTS	
Protein	
Carbohydrate – sugar (lactose)	
Fat	

VITAMINS	
Vitamin A – Retinol	Vitamin B7
Vitamin A – Carotene	Vitamin B9
Vitamin B1	Vitamin B12
Vitamin B2	Vitamin C
Vitamin B3	Vitamin D
Vitamin B5	Vitamin E

MINERALS	
Calcium	Manganese
Chloride	Phosphorus
Copper	Potassium
Iodine	Selenium
Iron	Sodium
Magnesium	Zinc

Water

Nutrient profile: fizzy lemonade

MACRONUTRIENTS
Carbohydrate (sugar: high fructose corn syrup)

VITAMINS
none

MINERALS
Calcium – small amount
Sodium – small amount

Water

Key learning: Modifying recipes, meals and diets to meet dietary guidelines

In your answers, you need to be able to explain how to modify a recipe, meal or diet to meet dietary guidelines and give examples

Base your meals on starchy foods

- Use wholegrain (wholemeal) cereal foods
- Choose a variety of starchy foods
- Add seeds to soups, stews, breads, desserts, porridge
- Toast starchy foods to add texture and flavour
- Add toasted seeds, rice flour, semolina to baked foods to add texture e.g. to biscuits, bread, pastries
- Roast starchy foods to strengthen flavour, e.g. sweet potatoes, butternut squash, carrots
- Serve bread with meals
- Serve food in wraps such as tortilla, pittas
- Dry fry seeds and sprinkle onto foods

Eat lots of fruit and vegetables

- Choose very fresh fruit and vegetables
- Choose locally produced and in season
- Add vegetables to main meals to increase the flavour, colour, texture
- Frozen fruit and vegetables are convenient and good
- Remove tough and inedible parts
- Garnish and decorate foods with fruit and vegetables

Eat more fish

- Fresh, frozen, dried, canned can be used (dried and canned may be salty)
- Choose sustainably sourced fish
- High-risk food
- Food hygiene and safety needs to be good when preparing fish
- Remove bones
- Flavour with lemon, lime, fresh herbs, fresh ginger, garlic
- Simple cooking method is best
- Often served with a sauce or dressing

Eat less saturated fat and sugar

- Study food labels for invisible fat and sugar in food products
- Eat fewer energy-dense foods, e.g. fried snacks, chocolate, biscuits, pastries, cakes, sweet fizzy drinks, sauces, salad dressings
- Eat more low energy foods, e.g. fruits and vegetables, wholemeal cereals
- Choose lean meat
- Cut down on meat products, e.g. sausages, pies, cold meats
- Choose low sugar and low fat versions of products
- Cut down on free (added) sugars
- Cut down on high fat foods, e.g. butter, cheese, lard, ghee
- Avoid frying food – grill, steam, or bake instead
- Use vegetables oils rather than solid fats
- Cut sugar content down in various recipes
- Trim fat from meat
- Avoid energy-dense accompaniments, e.g. cream, ice cream, custard, sauces

Eat less salt

- Read food labels for salt content
- Eat fewer salty snacks, e.g. crisps
- Eat fewer salty foods, e.g. cheese, canned or dried fish, processed meat products e.g. smoked bacon and sausages, salted nuts, yeast extract
- Choose low salt versions of food products
- Reduce or leave out salt from a recipe
- Reduce use of stock cubes
- Reduce consumption of ready meals and takeaway foods
- Use alternative flavours to salt e.g. lime juice, ginger, spices, garlic, spring onion
- Serve foods with alternatives to salt, e.g. fresh herbs, chillies, orange or lemon zest etc.

Nutrition Facts
Serving Size 5 oz. (144g)
Servings Per Container 4

Amount Per Serving

Calories 310	Calories fr... Fat ...
	% ... Value...
Total Fat 15g	17%
Saturated Fat 2.6g	17%
Trans Fat 1g	
Cholesterol 118mg	39%
Sodium 560mg	26%
Total Carbohydrate 12g	4%
Dietary Fiber 1g	5%
Sugars 1g	
Protein 24g	

| Vitamin A 1% | • | Vitamin C ...% |
| Calcium 2% | • | Iron 5% |

*Percent Daily Values are based on a 2,00... diet. Your daily values may be higher or lo... depending on your calorie needs:

	Calories	2,000	2,...
Total Fat	Less Than	65g	8...
Saturated Fat	Less Than	20g	2...
Cholesterol	Less Than	300mg	3...
Sodium	Less Than	2,400mg	2,...
Total Carbohydrate		300g	3...
Dietary Fiber		25g	30...

Calories per gram:
Fat 9 • Carbohydrate 4 • Protein 4

Key terms you should try to use in your answers

Modify: change something in a recipe, e.g. an ingredient or cooking method, to make it more suitable for current guidelines for a healthy diet

Nutrient profile: the different nutrients that a specific food contains

Activity 2.4

Suggest some ways in which you could reduce the energy density of the following food items/recipes by changing some of the ingredients and/or the method of cooking, to help someone who is trying to lose weight:

Name of recipe	Energy-dense ingredients	Change to ingredient or method of cooking
Quiche flan 	Shortcrust pastry	
	Cheddar cheese and cream in filling	
	Fried bacon in filling	
Cowboy pie (fried onions and baked beans on base then sausages then mashed potato with cheese on top) 	Base layer: fried onion with baked beans in tomato sauce	
	Middle layer: fried sausages	
	Topping: mashed potato with butter and grated cheese	
Trifle 	Base layer: sponge cake made with flour, eggs, sugar and butter	
	Custard: made with sugar and whole milk (full fat)	
	Topping: whipped double cream, grated chocolate and chopped nuts	
Tortilla wrap 	Filling: Fried chicken	
	Filling: Mayonnaise and avocado	

4 Diet, nutrition and health

Book-link:
1.2.4 Diet, nutrition and health, pages 70–77

What do you need to know?

You need to know:

- What is meant by good health
- How what we eat affects our health
- How diet-related diseases develop

Key learning: What is good health?

What does being in good health mean?

| Eating a healthy, balanced diet |

| Drinking plenty of water |

| Being physically active |

| Having enough sleep and relaxation |

| Avoiding too much stress |

Key learning: Diet-related diseases

What you must know about diet-related diseases

You need to know how to explain what causes diet-related diseases (risk factors) and the effects of each on the body

Further information you can add to extend your answers

Obesity

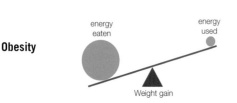

energy eaten — energy used

Weight gain

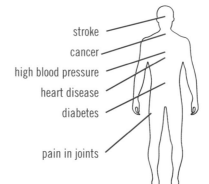

- stroke
- cancer
- high blood pressure
- heart disease
- diabetes
- pain in joints

- Many foods and soft drinks are energy dense and very palatable (tasty)
- Therefore, it is easy to consume a lot of them and gain weight over a period of time

Cardio-vascular disease (CVD)

high blood pressure

- High blood pressure damages the heart, blood vessels, eyes and kidneys
- It can cause a stroke (a blood clot in the brain)

Coronary heart disease (CHD)

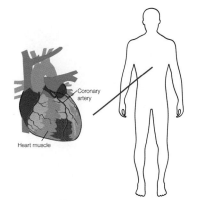

Coronary artery

Heart muscle

- Blood vessels in heart can become blocked by fatty deposits, which prevents oxygen reaching the heart muscle and causes a heart attack
- Antioxidants (vitamins A, C, and E) can help prevent CHD – eat lots of fresh fruit and vegetables

---

Skeletal disease

Lack of vitamin D and calcium

Rickets (children)

Osteomalacia (adults)

Natural ageing process where minerals are removed from the skeleton which gradually weakens

Osteoporosis

- Need to reach peak bone mass by age 35 years to make sure the skeleton is as strong as possible

---

Tooth decay

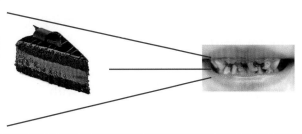

- Caused by bacteria in mouth turning sugars and other foods into acids
- The acids dissolve outside layer of tooth (the enamel) and cause decay
- Avoid sweetened fizzy drinks and fruit juices which are acidic and can dissolve the enamel

---

Iron deficiency anaemia

- Not enough haemoglobin in red blood cells made so not enough oxygen carried round the body to produce energy

- Caused by a lack of iron (or vitamin C, which is needed to absorb iron)
- Teenage girls and women more likely to be anaemic due to menstruation
- Symptoms are tiredness, no energy, muscle weakness, feeling cold

---

Type 2 diabetes

Blood vessels damaged

Eye damage

Kidney damage

Nerve endings damaged

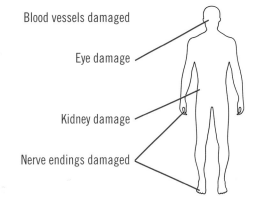

- Increasing numbers of younger people are developing Type 2 diabetes
- Caused by glucose not being able to get into body cells to produce energy
- Due to lack of insulin being produced in the pancreas or unable to be used by the body
- Symptoms include thirst, urinating frequently, weight loss, tiredness and weakness, blurred vision
- Permanent damage is done to small blood vessels, nerve endings, eyes and skin

Applying your learning

A middle-aged man has been told by his doctor that his blood pressure is too high and has been advised to reduce the amount of salt he eats.

- Suggest four ways in which he can flavour his food to make it appetising, without using salt.

- Explain why he should also reduce his consumption of foods that contain baking powder, soy sauce, cheese, bacon and ham.

Key terms you should try to use in your answers

Risk factor: an action or a natural tendency that makes you more likely to develop a disease or health condition

Malnutrition: having a diet that is not balanced

Diet-related disease: a disease or health condition where one or more of the risk factors for developing it are what or how much of particular foods or beverages (drinks) you eat or drink over a period of time

Activity 2.5

Solve the puzzle below by filling in the missing letters. The clues are in the questions:

H _ _ _   blood pressure is a **risk factor** for heart disease

E _ _ _ _ _ _ _   is important for preventing heart disease

A _ _ _ _ _ _ _ _ _ _   (vitamins A, C and E) can help prevent heart disease

R _ _ _ _ _ _ _   stress levels can lower the risk of developing heart disease

T _ _   much salt raises blood pressure

D _ _ _ _ _ _   guidelines should be followed to help prevent heart disease

I _ _ _ _ _ _ _   people who sit about a lot are at risk of developing heart disease

S _ _ _ _ _   is a risk factor for heart disease

E _ _ _ _ _ _ _   helps to strengthen the heart

A _ _ _ _ _ _ _   in the heart muscle can become blocked with fatty deposits

S _ _ _ _ _ _ _ _   fats can raise blood cholesterol levels and cause blockages in the arteries

E _ _ _ _ _   body weight puts a big strain on the heart

Multiple choice challenge

Have a go at answering these questions. They are worth **one mark** each. Answers are on page 145.

1. **The definition of the word 'diet' is:**
   - a) The food you should eat to lose weight
   - b) The food you eat every day
   - c) The food you should eat when you visit another country
   - d) The food you should only eat when you are an adult

2. **One of the dietary guidelines recommends:**
   - a) Eat less salt – no more than 2g a day for adults
   - b) Eat less salt – no more than 5g a day for adults
   - c) Eat less salt – no more than 6g a day for adults
   - d) Eat less salt – no more than 8g a day for adults

3. **The Eatwell Guide applies to:**
   - a) Everyone
   - b) 6-month-old babies
   - c) Children from 1 to 2 years
   - d) Children over the age of 5 years and adults

4. **The Eatwell Guide recommends that the consumption of fruit juice and / or smoothies should be limited to:**
   - a) 1.5 mls a day
   - b) 150 mls a day
   - c) 1 litre a day
   - d) 1.5 litres a day

5. **Young children and teenagers should be encouraged to:**
   - [ ] a) Eat regular meals especially breakfast
   - [ ] b) Drink unsweetened drinks
   - [ ] c) Eat fresh and raw foods
   - [ ] d) All of these

6. **A coeliac diet must be free from:**
   - [ ] a) Glucose
   - [ ] b) Glycerine
   - [ ] c) Gluten
   - [ ] d) Guava

7. **Lacto-vegetarians can eat:**
   - [ ] a) Dairy products, all plant foods and eggs
   - [ ] b) Dairy products, all plant foods, eggs and fish
   - [ ] c) Dairy products, all plant foods, and chicken
   - [ ] d) Dairy products, all plant foods

8. **Energy-dense foods usually contain a lot of:**
   - [ ] a) Fat and/or sugar
   - [ ] b) Water
   - [ ] c) Water and protein
   - [ ] d) Fat and/or salt

9. **Energy balance means that:**
   - [ ] a) The amount of energy eaten in food is less than the amount of energy used
   - [ ] b) The amount of energy eaten in food is the same as the amount of energy used
   - [ ] c) The amount of energy eaten in food is more than the amount of energy used
   - [ ] d) The amount of energy eaten in food is twice the amount of energy used

10. **Dietary guidelines recommend that the percentage of energy from different nutrients should be:**
    - [ ] a) Carbohydrate 60%, Fat 25% or less, Protein 15% per day
    - [ ] b) Sugars 50%, Fat 35% or less, Protein 15% per day
    - [ ] c) Carbohydrate 50%, Fat 35% or more, Protein 15% per day
    - [ ] d) Carbohydrate 50%, Fat 35% or less, Protein 15% per day

11. **The risk factors for coronary heart disease are:**
    - [ ] a) Being active, obese, eating too much salt and saturated fats
    - [ ] b) Being inactive, obese, eating too much salt and saturated fats
    - [ ] c) Being inactive, obese, eating too much salt and fruits and vegetables
    - [ ] d) Being inactive, lacking vitamin D, eating too much salt and saturated fats

12. **Tooth decay is caused by:**
    - [ ] a) Acids produced by bacteria breaking down proteins in the mouth
    - [ ] b) Acids produced by bacteria breaking down sugars and starches in the mouth
    - [ ] c) Acids produced by bacteria breaking down saliva in the mouth
    - [ ] d) Alkalis produced by bacteria breaking down sugars and starches in the mouth

13. **The name given to the natural ageing process where the bones become porous and weaken is:**
    - [ ] a) Anaemia
    - [ ] b) Rickets
    - [ ] c) Osteoporosis
    - [ ] d) Peak bone mass

14. **Anaemia is the name given to a deficiency of:**
    - [ ] a) Iodine
    - [ ] b) Iron
    - [ ] c) Fluoride
    - [ ] d) Phosphorus

15. **Some people cannot drink milk because they are:**
    - [ ] a) Lipid intolerant
    - [ ] b) Gluten intolerant
    - [ ] c) Glucose intolerant
    - [ ] d) Lactose intolerant

16. **The following foods all have a high salt content:**
    - [ ] a) Cheese, fresh vegetables, milk and yeast extract
    - [ ] b) Cheese, chutney, smoked bacon and yeast extract
    - [ ] c) Cheese, honey, smoked bacon and yeast extract
    - [ ] d) Cheese, soy sauce, fresh vegetables and yeast extract

17. **BMR stands for:**
    - [ ] a) Basic metabolic reaction
    - [ ] b) Basal movement rate
    - [ ] c) Basal metabolic rate
    - [ ] d) Best metabolic rate

18. **Some people cannot eat bread made from wheat because they are:**
    - [ ] a) Lipid intolerant
    - [ ] b) Gluten intolerant
    - [ ] c) Glucose intolerant
    - [ ] d) Lactose intolerant

19. **The following foods all have a high free sugar content:**
    - [ ] a) Cheese, fresh vegetables, milk and jam
    - [ ] b) Honey, chutney, chocolate spread and yeast extract
    - [ ] c) Chocolate spread, honey, jam and ice cream
    - [ ] d) Chocolate spread, honey, soy sauce and tomato ketchup

20. **PAL stands for:**
    - [ ] a) Physical action level
    - [ ] b) Physical activity level
    - [ ] c) Physical activity label
    - [ ] d) Partial activity level

Knowledge check – can you recall...?

(Answers on pages 146–148)

1. The eight dietary guidelines? *(8 marks)*
2. What the word 'diet' means? *(1 mark)*
3. The names of five special diets? *(5 marks)*
4. What a healthy balanced diet means? *(1 mark)*
5. Five general rules for planning meals for anyone? *(5 marks)*
6. Three best eating habits and lifestyle choices for children aged 1–4 years? *(3 marks)*
7. Three best eating habits and lifestyle choices for children aged 5–12 years? *(3 marks)*
8. Three best eating habits and lifestyle choices for teenagers? *(3 marks)*
9. Three best eating habits and lifestyle choices for adults? *(3 marks)*
10. Three best eating habits and lifestyle choices for elderly adults? *(3 marks)*
11. Why iron and vitamin C are especially important for teenage girls and adult women? *(1 mark)*
12. Why calcium and vitamin D are especially important for teenagers and adults? *(2 marks)*
13. Why protein is especially important for young children? *(1 mark)*
14. Why vitamins A, C and E are especially important for elderly adults? *(1 mark)*
15. Two foods that lacto-vegetarians do eat and two that they do not? *(4 marks)*
16. Two foods that a coeliac can eat and two that they cannot? *(4 marks)*
17. Two foods that someone on a low sodium diet can eat and two that they should not? *(4 marks)*
18. Three reasons why the body needs energy? *(3 marks)*
19. What an energy-dense food is? *(1 mark)*
20. The main source of energy for the body? *(1 mark)*
21. What happens to the body if you have excess energy from food? *(1 mark)*
22. What BMR means and what its definition is? *(2 marks)*
23. Two reasons why physical activity is important for the body? *(2 marks)*
24. Three possible effects on the body of being obese? *(3 marks)*
25. Three possible effects on the body of having Type 2 diabetes? *(3 marks)*
26. Three possible effects on the body of having high blood pressure obese? *(3 marks)*
27. Three risk factors that may lead to the development of coronary heart disease? *(3 marks)*
28. How tooth decay develops? *(3 marks)*
29. Two types of foods / drinks to avoid in order to prevent tooth decay? *(2 marks)*
30. Three symptoms of iron deficiency anaemia? *(3 marks)*

Stretch and challenge questions

The Eatwell Guide gives advice to people about how to choose a healthy, balanced diet.

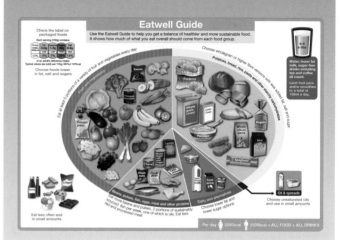

1. Explain in detail, the reasons for the following pieces of advice given on the Eatwell Guide:

   a) Starchy foods: Choose wholegrain or higher fibre versions with less added fat, salt and sugar. *(4 marks)*

   b) Oils and spreads: Choose unsaturated oils and use in small amounts. *(4 marks)*

   c) Eat more beans and pulses, two portions of sustainably sourced fish per week, one of which is oily. Eat less red and processed meats. *(4 marks)*

2. In the UK, the number of people changing from a meat eating to a vegetarian diet has grown over the past few years.

   a) Analyse the reasons why more people are choosing to eat a vegetarian diet, giving details and examples in your answer. *(5 marks)*

   b) Explain the similarities and differences between a lacto-ovo vegetarian diet and a vegan diet. *(3 marks)*

3. The number of people who develop osteoporosis is rising each year in the UK.

   a) Explain what osteoporosis is and why it develops. *(4 marks)*

   b) Explain why it is important that young people know about osteoporosis and what they can do to help prevent themselves from developing it when they are older. *(4 marks)*

Chapter 3: Cooking of food and heat transfer

Reasons why food is cooked

Book-link:
2.1.1 Why food is cooked and how heat is transferred to food, pages 78–90

What do you need to know?

You now know about which foods make up healthy balanced diets for different life stages and dietary needs.

Next you need to know:

- The reasons why food is **cooked**
- The different methods of **transferring heat** to food: **conduction**, **convection** and **radiation**
- Different **cooking methods**
- How cooking affects the **sensory qualities**, **palatability** and **nutritional value** of foods
- How to **conserve** (prevent from being lost) certain nutrients in foods

Here is a revision mind map to help you learn about the reasons why food is cooked:

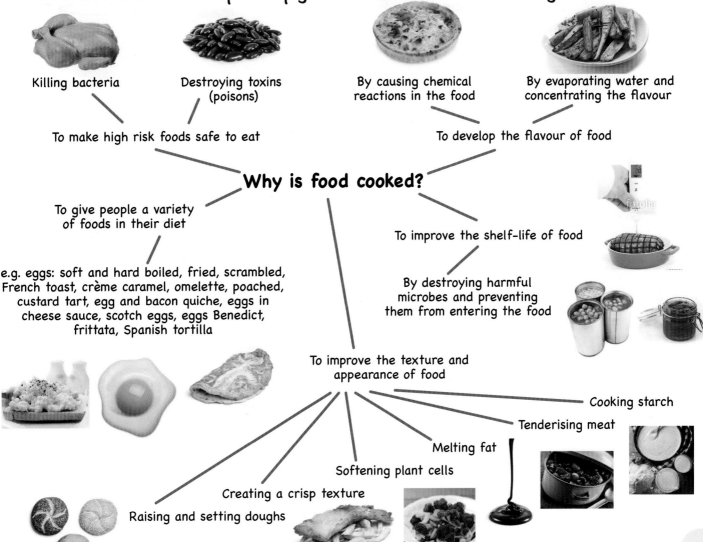

Killing bacteria

Destroying toxins (poisons)

By causing chemical reactions in the food

By evaporating water and concentrating the flavour

To make high risk foods safe to eat

To develop the flavour of food

Why is food cooked?

To give people a variety of foods in their diet

e.g. eggs: soft and hard boiled, fried, scrambled, French toast, crème caramel, omelette, poached, custard tart, egg and bacon quiche, eggs in cheese sauce, scotch eggs, eggs Benedict, frittata, Spanish tortilla

To improve the shelf-life of food

By destroying harmful microbes and preventing them from entering the food

To improve the texture and appearance of food

Cooking starch

Tenderising meat

Melting fat

Softening plant cells

Creating a crisp texture

Raising and setting doughs

2

Different methods of transferring heat to food

Book-link:
2.1.1 Why food is cooked and how heat is transferred to food, pages 85–90

Cooking of food and heat transfer

Key learning: Different methods of transferring heat to food

Conduction

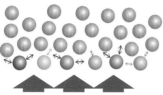 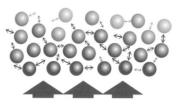 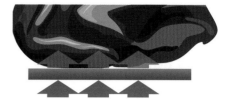

Atoms in metal pans and baking trays start to vibrate as heat energy from the hob or oven goes into the metal

The vibrations transfer heat energy to other metal atoms

The metal gradually heats up and passes the heat energy into the food

Metals are **good conductors of heat** – very good for baked products

Plastic/wood/air/thick cotton or wool are **good heat insulators** (poor conductors of heat) – so they are used for pan handles, oven gloves, wooden spoons, etc., to protect the hands

Convection

As a pan of water is heated, heat is conducted through the metal pan to the water molecules

Water molecules then move upwards then downwards in a circular motion (convection currents) taking heat energy with them and passing it on to the food

The more heat energy the faster the water molecules and convection currents move

Convection also happens in ovens with **hot air currents**.

Gas ovens/ordinary electric ovens have **zones of heat –** i.e. they are **hotter on the top shelf** than the bottom shelf due to convection.

The heat in **electric fan ovens** is evenly distributed by a fan, so it is the same temperature on each shelf.

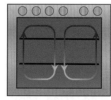 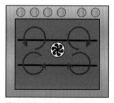

Gas oven/ordinary electric oven

Electric fan oven

Radiation

3.5cm

Grilled/barbequed food is heated by **radiant heat**, which heats objects it comes into contact with.

Infrared heat rays heat the surface of the food and are absorbed

Food must be **no more than 3.5cm thick** otherwise it may be under-cooked inside

Food must not be too close to the grill/barbeque or it may easily burn

3 Different methods of cooking

Book-link:
2.1.2 Selecting appropriate cooking methods, pages 90–101

Key learning: Different methods of cooking

In your answers, you need to know how to explain:

What you must know about different cooking methods	The method of heat transfer in each cooking method	The effects and scientific principles of the cooking method on different ingredients	The effects of the cooking method on the sensory qualities of foods and palatability (flavour, aroma [smell], texture, appearance)	The effects of the cooking method on different nutrients

Moist cooking methods – water is used to transfer heat energy to the food:
• Boiling
• Braising
• Poaching
• Simmering
• Steaming
• Stewing
	• Conduction
	↓
	• Convection
		• Starch absorbs water and gelatinises
		• Proteins denature and coagulate – become solid
		• Fat melts
		• Water evaporates – sauces reduce (thicken)
		• Colours change, e.g.:
		  – meat from red to brown
		  – vegetables become bright green
			• Vegetables, fruits, pasta, rice, etc., tenderise
			• Meat tenderises (collagen converts to gelatine) – can become tough and indigestible if overcooked
			• Flavour intensifies
				• Vitamins B1, B2 and C dissolve in water and are gradually destroyed by heat
				• Vitamins B1, B2 and C can be **conserved** by:
				  – preparing, cutting, grating, squeezing and cooking just before serving
				  – using only a little water
				  – limiting their exposure to light and oxygen
				  – serving foods as soon as they are cooked
				  – use the water the vegetables were cooked in to make gravy or soup

Methods where oil is used to transfer heat energy to the food: • Sautéing • Shallow/pan frying • Stir frying • Roasting • Deep fat frying	• Conduction ↓ • Convection	• Intrinsic (natural) sugars caramelise and make food go a golden colour, e.g. sautéed onions • Starch absorbs oil and swells • Protein denatures and coagulates • Meat shrinks and squeezes out juices • Energy density of food is increased by the oil being absorbed into the food	• Flavour of foods intensifies as water evaporates • Vegetables/fruits soften • Foods become crisp on the outside – especially if coated with egg and breadcrumbs to protect the food from the heat of the oil	Vitamins B1, B2 and C are gradually destroyed by the heat of the oil

Methods where dry heat is used to transfer heat energy to the food: • Baking • Grilling • Toasting • Dry frying	Baking: • Convection ↓ • Conduction Grilling: • Radiation Dry frying: • Conduction	• Gases from raising agents expand and make food rise • Starch on the outside turns to dextrin and goes golden brown • Protein denatures and coagulates – overcooking makes it less digestible • Meat proteins in muscle cells shrink and squeeze out juices • Free sugars melt and soften gluten in the flour • Sugars caramelise • Fat melts and is released from meats – reduces energy density • Starch granules absorb water/fat and swell and soften • Gluten stretches as doughs rise then sets around gas bubbles	Starch becomes more digestible Flavours intensify	Vitamins B1, B2 and C are gradually destroyed by the intense heat
• Microwaving	• Radiation: - electromagnetic waves **vibrate water molecules** in food - this produces heat energy which is transferred very quickly to the rest of the food	• Protein denatures and coagulates quickly • Fat melts • Sugar caramelises and will burn easily • Starch gelatinises • Juices and water from meat are easily squeezed out	Protein will quickly overcook and become tough and indigestible	A little damage to vitamins B1, B2 and C
Using an induction hob: • Boiling • Frying • Poaching • Stewing	• Conduction	Same as for moist cooking methods	Same as for moist cooking methods	Same as for moist cooking methods

Revision tip

Try to remember at least four different foods that are suitable to be cooked by each cooking method.

Choose a food, e.g. eggs, cheese, apples, rice, and make a list of all the different ways in which it can be cooked and the effects of different cooking methods on its sensory properties.

Learn to draw and annotate diagrams to show the different methods of heat transfer.

Key terms you should try to use in your answers

Heat transfer: the way in which heat energy is passed into food

Conduction: transferring heat through a solid object into food

Convection: transferring heat through a liquid or air into food

Radiation: transferring heat by infrared waves that heat up what they come into contact with a solid object

Palatability: what makes a food acceptable and good to eat

Sensory qualities: the characteristics of a food that give it a particular appearance, flavour, texture, 'mouthfeel' (what it feels like, not what it tastes like, when you put it in your mouth), aroma (smell) and sound (some foods are crunchy, crispy or crackly and make a sound when they are cooked or eaten)

Here are some revision mind maps to help you learn about which foods are suitable for different cooking methods

Activity 3.1

Look at the different cooking methods below and explain which heat transfer method is used to cook the food.

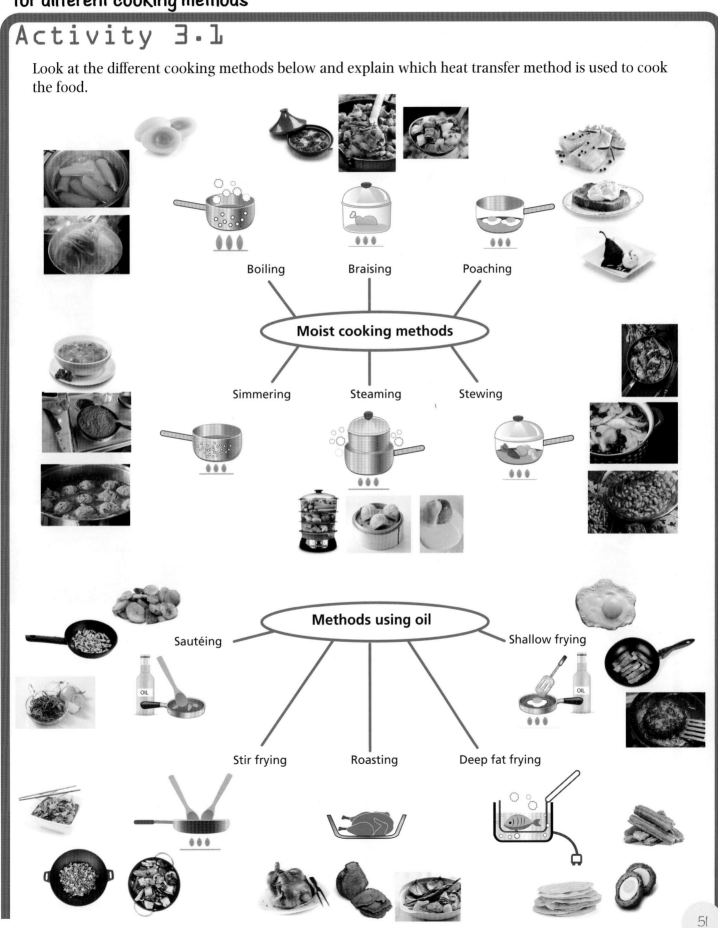

Cooking of food and heat transfer

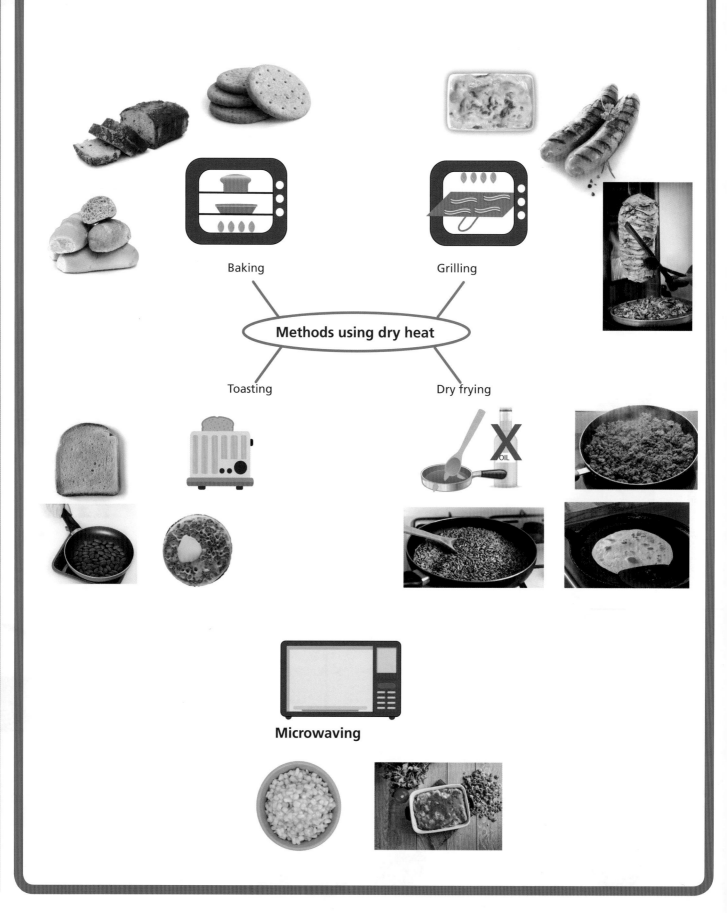

Baking

Grilling

Methods using dry heat

Toasting

Dry frying

OIL

Microwaving

Activity 3.2

Look at the method below which is for a vegetable and pasta medley recipe (book-link: pages 40 – 41).

Identify and list the **cooking methods** and methods of **heat transfer** that are used in this recipe. Explain how each method will affect the **sensory qualities** and **palatability** of the ingredients used:

Explain your understanding of the **functional** and **chemical properties** of the different stages/cooking of the ingredients.

Method	Cooking method used and method of heat transfer involved	Effects on the sensory qualities of the ingredients
1. Heat the oven: • Gas 6/200°C (190°C if you are using a fan oven). **2. Vegetables:** • Spread the vegetables on a metal tray and drizzle the oil over them. • Add the seasoning and place the vegetables in the oven for 25–30 minutes, turning them occasionally until browned and tender.	Baking	
3. Pasta: • Place the pasta in a large pan of boiling water and cook until it is tender. Drain it using a sieve or colander.	Bioling	
4. Cheese sauce: • Grate the cheese onto a plate. *All-in-one method:* • Put the flour and the mustard powder in a mixing bowl. • Gradually add the milk, mixing it to make it smooth with a wooden spoon or balloon whisk. • Add the butter. • Place the bowl into the microwave and set the timer to 1 minute. • When it **stops, stir the sauce thoroughly and microwave again for 1 minute – stir the sauce again.** • Repeat this 4–5 times until the sauce has thickened and is smooth and glossy. • Take it out of the microwave and add ¾ of the grated cheese. Stir until the cheese has melted.		

Béchamel (roux) method:

- In a small saucepan, melt the butter on the hob – do not let it burn.

- Add the flour and mustard and continue heating it, stirring it all the time with a wooden spoon, for 1 minute (roux).

- Remove the pan from the heat.

- Gradually add the milk to the roux, stirring well each time to avoid any lumps forming, until all the milk has been added.

- Put the pan back on the heat and, stirring all the time, heat the sauce until it boils and thickens – the sauce should coat the back of the wooden spoon and be smooth and glossy in appearance.

- Remove the pan from the heat and add ¾ of the grated cheese. Stir until the cheese has melted.

5. Assemble the dish

- Put the vegetables and the cooked pasta into the dish, then pour the sauce over.

- Topping

- Sprinkle the rest of the cheese on top.

- Place the dish under a hot grill and heat until golden brown on top.

Activity 3.3

Look at the mind map below, which shows how potatoes can be prepared in lots of different ways to give people a variety of foods in their diet.

In each of the blank spaces, write down the name of the cooking method that you think has been used to cook the potatoes. Some of them may have more than one cooking method:

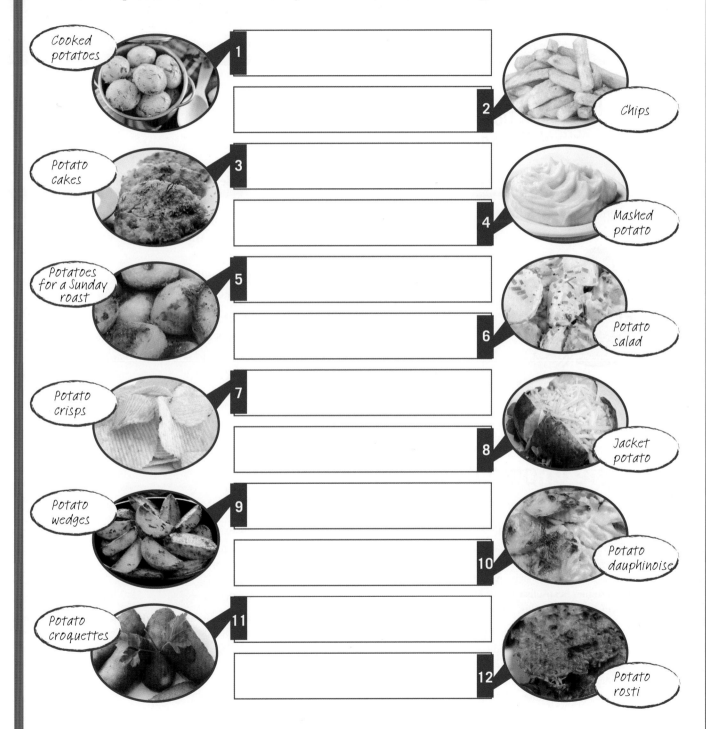

Answer the questions below:

1. Explain what happens to the sensory qualities of potatoes when they are cooked by different methods.
2. Explain why some of the potatoes in the pictures have a golden brown colour on the outside.

Applying your learning

You are making a Bolognese sauce using minced beef. The recipe tells you to shallow fry the meat in some oil before adding the other ingredients.

- Explain how you could reduce the fat content of the Bolognese sauce by changing the cooking method for the minced beef. Give reasons for your answer.

Applying your learning

You are preparing a meal of roasted chicken, potatoes, broccoli, green cabbage, carrots, and peas.

- Explain how you will prepare, cook and serve the vegetables in order to conserve as many of their nutrients as possible.

Give reasons for your answers.

THEORY INTO PRACTICE
– try this practical challenge

Plan and make a two-course meal for two adults that uses at least five different cooking methods.

QUESTIONS

Using your knowledge and understanding of the sensory properties of foods:

1. Explain how the different cooking methods you have used will affect the sensory properties of the ingredients in your chosen meal. *(5 marks)*

2. Describe how changing the method of cooking could improve the nutritional profile for each of the following meals:

   a) Deep fried fish and chips. *(1 mark)*

   b) Shallow fried beef burgers and thin potato fries. *(1 mark)*

   c) Deep fried battered sweet and sour prawns and fried rice. *(1 mark)*

Multiple choice challenge

Have a go at answering these questions. They are worth **one mark** each. Answers are on page 145.

1. **Food is cooked to make the following high risk foods safe to eat:**
   a) Sausages, biscuits, fish, minced beef
   [X] b) Chicken, red kidney beans, fish, minced beef
   c) Pork, runner beans, fish, minced beef
   d) Turkey burgers, biscuits, bread, cheese

2. **The following are all moist methods of cooking:**
   a) Sautéing, simmering, steaming, stewing
   b) Braising, boiling, baking, barbequing
   [X] c) Simmering, steaming, braising, stewing
   d) Braising, boiling, sautéing and stewing

3. **The method of heat transfer in roasting is:**
   a) Conduction to convection
   [X] b) Convection to conduction
   c) Convection to radiation
   d) Conduction to radiation

4. **Dry heat causes the following reaction in baked products:**
   a) Denaturation
   b) Decomposition
   c) Dehydration
   [X] d) Dextrinisation

5. **Moist cooking methods cause the following reaction in foods containing starch:**
   [X] a) Gelatinisation
   b) Dextrinisation
   c) Caramelisation
   d) Dehydration

6. **Roasting vegetables has the following effects on their sensory properties:**
   a) Flavour weakens and natural sugars caramelise
   b) Flavour weakens because oil is added
   c) Flavour concentrates and natural sugars caramelise
   d) Flavour concentrates and vegetables swell in size

7. Vitamin C can be conserved when preparing and cooking vegetables by:
- a) Preparing and cooking just before serving
- b) Keeping the vegetables hot for 20 minutes before serving
- c) Soaking the vegetables in water for 30 minutes before cooking
- d) Boiling vegetables in a lot of water

8. When meat is stewed, it becomes tender because:
- a) Gluten converts to gelatine
- b) Collagen converts to gluten
- c) Gelatine converts to collagen
- d) Collagen converts to gelatine

9. Microwaving heats food by causing:
- a) Starch molecules to give up heat energy
- b) Water molecules to vibrate and give off heat energy
- c) Water molecules to evaporate
- d) Starch molecules to vibrate and give off heat energy

10. The heat transfer involved in grilling is:
- a) Infra-green radiation
- b) Electromagnetic waves
- c) Infrared radiation
- d) Infrared reduction

Knowledge check – can you recall...?
(Answers on page 148)

1. What electromagnetic waves in microwaving do? *(1 mark)*
2. The names of the cooking methods where dry heat is used to transfer heat energy to food? *(4 marks)*
3. The names of the cooking methods where oil is used to transfer heat energy to food? *(5 marks)*
4. The names of the cooking methods where moisture is used to transfer heat energy to food? *(6 marks)*
5. Five foods that are suitable to be cooked by moist cooking methods? *(5 marks)*
6. Three foods that are suitable to be cooked by dry heat methods? *(3 marks)*
7. What happens to starch when it is heated in moisture? *(2 marks)*
8. What happens to minced beef when it is cooked by dry frying? *(2 marks)*
9. What happens to meat or fish if they are cooked for too long under a grill? *(2 marks)*
10. Four ways of conserving the vitamins in vegetables? *(4 marks)*
11. Why gas and ordinary electric ovens have zones of heat? *(2 marks)*
12. Why foods can be baked evenly on any shelf in an electric fan oven? *(2 marks)*
13. Why microwaving heats food very quickly? *(2 marks)*
14. Why cakes, pastries, biscuits, scones, etc., develop a golden brown crust when baked in the oven? *(2 marks)*
15. Why stir frying is considered to be a healthier method of cooking than shallow frying? *(1 mark)*

Stretch and challenge questions

1. Explain, giving detailed reasons:
   a) Which method of cooking you would use to cook a piece of meat which includes lots of muscle (is a tougher cut of meat). *(4 marks)*
   b) How the beef would become tender. *(4 marks)*

2. Using your knowledge of cooking methods and heat transfer, explain in detail, the reasons for the following instructions:
   a) Pieces of meat and poultry that are to be grilled should be no thicker than 3.5cm. *(2 marks)*
   b) Boil raw kidney beans for at least 15 minutes. *(2 marks)*
   c) Coat raw fish or chicken in flour, egg and breadcrumbs or batter before deep frying. *(2 marks)*

3. Explain in detail, the effects on the sensory properties, palatability and nutritional value of the following foods by the three different cooking methods shown for each:
   a) Broccoli – cooked by steaming, stir frying and microwaving. *(4 marks)*
   b) Potatoes – cooked by boiling, baking and roasting. *(4 marks)*
   c) White fish – cooked by shallow frying, baking and poaching. *(4 marks)*

Chapter 4: Functional and chemical properties of food

What do you need to know?

You now know why foods are cooked, how heat is transferred and different methods of cooking foods.

Next you need to know:

- What different ingredients do in recipes (their **functional properties**)
- How and why different ingredients react and change when they are prepared and cooked (their **chemical properties**)
- What happens to the **appearance**, **colour**, **texture** and flavour of the food in a recipe when it is prepared and cooked
- How to choose the best cooking method for different foods
- Why raising agents are used and how they work in different foods

1 Proteins

Book-link:
2.2.1 Proteins, pages 105–115

What you must know about the food science of protein

In your answers, you need to know how to explain the food science involved (the functional and chemical properties of protein)

Further information you can add to extend your answers:

The **chemical structure** of protein	• Protein molecules are **very big** • They are made of long chains of **amino acids** and formed into bundles held together by **chemical bonds**	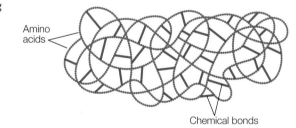 Amino acids Chemical bonds
What **denaturation** means	The chemical bonds in protein molecules can be **broken** by: • Heating food • Mechanical agitation, e.g. whisking eggs/eggs and sugar • Adding acids, e.g. lemon juice/tomato juice added to raw meat to tenderise it (marinating) • Air bubbles, e.g. formed in meringue	• Protein molecule bundles unfold and change shape as the bonds break – they **denature**  Broken chemical bonds

What **coagulation** means	• As protein foods are prepared and cooked, they change texture and become more **solid (set),** e.g. eggs, meat, fish • Denatured protein molecules unfold and join up with other ones to form big groups – they **coagulate** • As they coagulate, they trap air and water	• Overcooking causes the coagulated protein molecules to tighten up and squeeze out the trapped water – the food will become dry and tough, e.g. overcooked meat, overcooked scrambled egg 
How **gluten** is formed and why it is important in baked mixtures	• **Gluten** (in wheat flour) is an important protein for producing the right **texture** in baked products, e.g. breads, cakes, pastries, biscuits • Gluten makes doughs **stretchy** and **elastic** and able to be **shaped** and **rise** • Gluten **traps gas bubbles** that have been produced in the dough, e.g. in bread making • Doughs will often shrink back when they are stretched, e.g. shortcrust and puff pastry doughs • Gluten lets doughs **rise** as the **gas bubbles** they contain **expand** during baking • Gluten **coagulates** and **sets** the baked mixture in the last stages of baking	• **Gluten** in wheat flour is formed from 2 proteins called **glutenin** and **gliadin** when water is added to flour ▶ 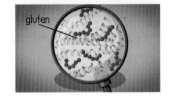    • Pastry dough should be rested to allow the gluten to relax so it does not shrink fast in the oven
How **foams** are formed	• Egg white protein can **stretch and hold** a large volume of **air** to produce a **foam,** e.g. meringue • Air is trapped in a **gas-in-liquid foam** by whisking, e.g. egg whites for **meringue** or eggs and sugar for **whisked sponges** (e.g. Swiss roll)	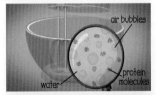 • The whisking action denatures the protein 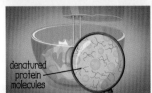 • The denatured proteins coagulate and surround air bubbles

Key terms you should try to use in your answers

Chemical bonds: bonds that hold large protein molecules together in compact, folded bundles

Denaturation: the chemical bonds have broken and the protein molecule has unfolded and changed shape

Coagulation: the joining together of lots of denatured protein molecules, which changes the appearance and texture of the food

Gluten: formed from two separate proteins: glutenin and gliadin, which combine when liquid is added to flour to make a dough

Revision tip

If you find it difficult to remember some of the food science terms (words) try some of the following tips to help you:

- Use a highlighter pen in your revision notes to make the words stand out

- Make a glossary (list) of words and their meanings and pin it up where you can easily see it

- Draw some diagrams to show what each word means

- Read the word and its meaning, cover it with your hand and repeat it several times

- When you are cooking at home or at school, describe to someone what is happening when the food cooks using the correct food science terms

- Annotate all the recipes you make explaining which food science terms are used (there is an activity later in this chapter to help you do this)

- Create a set of revision cards/word game and the science terms and meanings. Test your friends with the game.

Applying your learning

You are making a whisked sponge for a Swiss roll.

1. Explain why the flour must be <u>very carefully</u> added to the whisked egg and sugar foam.

2. What will make the Swiss roll rise and then set in the oven?

3. Draw a diagram of the Swiss roll and annotate the functional and chemical processes that have happened to achieve the perfect result.

Applying your learning

You are making some scrambled eggs in a pan.

1. Explain why you have to control the heat very carefully and not cook the eggs for too long.

2. Describe what the appearance and texture of the scrambled eggs will be like if they are overcooked. Explain why this would happen.

Applying your learning

You are making some bread rolls.

1. Why should you use strong plain flour to make the bread rolls?

2. Explain why you must make sure you have added the right amount of water to the dough.

3. Why must you knead the dough for several minutes?

4. Why does the bread roll rise and then set in the oven?

Activity 4.1

Explain (using the correct food science terms) what is happening to the egg in the pictures below:

  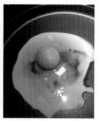 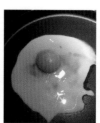 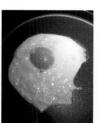 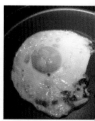

2 Carbohydrates

Book-link:
2.2.2 Carbohydrates, pages 116–125

What you must know about the food science of carbohydrates

In your answers, you need to know how to explain the food science involved (the functional and chemical properties of carbohydrates)

Further information you can add to extend your answers:

Where starch is found

- Starch is made by plants and stored in their roots, fruits and seeds
- Starch is found inside small 'packets' called **granules** inside the plant
- Starch granules, e.g. in flour, sink to the bottom of cold liquids

- Sauces must be stirred all the time to prevent starch granules sticking together on the bottom of the pan and making lumps

How starch reacts when heated in a liquid and in dry heat

- When heated to **60°C** starch granules absorb water and swell up

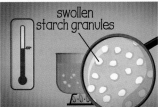

- At **80°C** starch granules are very swollen and start to burst, letting starch out into the liquid

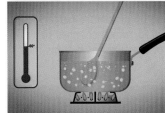

- At **100°C** the liquid completely thickens – it has **gelatinised**

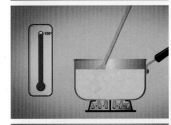
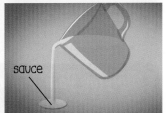

- As it cools it becomes a solid gel
- The whole process is called **gelatinisation**

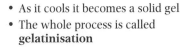

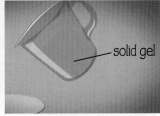

- The starch molecules form a 3D network that traps water

- Baked and toasted (grilled) foods that contain starch develop a golden brown crust on the outside, e.g. toasted bread.
- This is called **dextrinisation**

- **Dry heat** (oven/grill) causes starch to change colour, texture and flavour
- Starch changes to **dextrin**

How sugar reacts when heated	• Sugars are made by plants and some are stored in fruits, seeds, stems, and roots	• There are several types of sugar, e.g.: sucrose, fructose, glucose, maltose
	• **Sucrose** is the sugar mainly used in cooking	• Foods that contain natural sugars, e.g. onions, carrots, parsnips, will **caramelise** when fried or roasted
	• When sugar (sucrose) is heated it melts to a **syrup**, which boils	• Different sugars that are found in different foods often appear on the ingredients lists of food product labels, e.g. sucrose, maltose, fructose, glucose, dextrose, lactose. They all end in 'ose', which will help consumers to recognise them.
	• The **sucrose molecules** break up and **water molecules** are formed	
	• The water **evaporates**, the syrup gets thicker and changes to a golden brown colour (**caramel**)	• It will eventually burn and become bitter if cooked for too long
	• The process is called **caramelisation**	

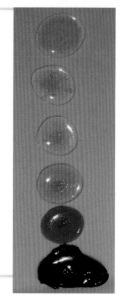

Key terms you should try to use in your answers

Gelatinisation: the swelling of starch granules when they are cooked with a liquid to the point where they burst and release starch molecules

Dextrinisation: the breaking up of starch molecules into smaller groups of glucose molecules when they are exposed to dry heat

Caramelisation: the breaking up of sucrose (sugar) molecules when they are heated, which changes the colour, flavour and texture of the sugar as it turns into caramel

Applying your learning

You are making a caramel sauce.

1. Explain why you must not stir the caramel while it is heating.

2. Explain why you must not allow the caramel to turn dark brown when making it.

3. Explain why you must be very safety conscious when making caramel.

Applying your learning

You are making a béchamel sauce for a pasta and cheese sauce recipe.

1. Which ingredient in the sauce contains starch?

2. Explain how the sauce thickens.

3. Explain why you must stir the sauce all the time while it is cooking in the pan.

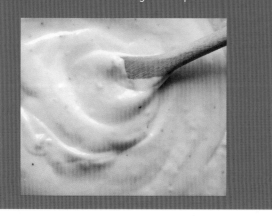

Applying your learning

You are making a savoury cheese and caramelised onion scone.

1. Explain why the outside of the scone changes to a golden brown colour.

2. Explain why the onions change to a golden brown colour when they are sautéed.

Here is a revision mind map to help you learn about the science of carbohydrates

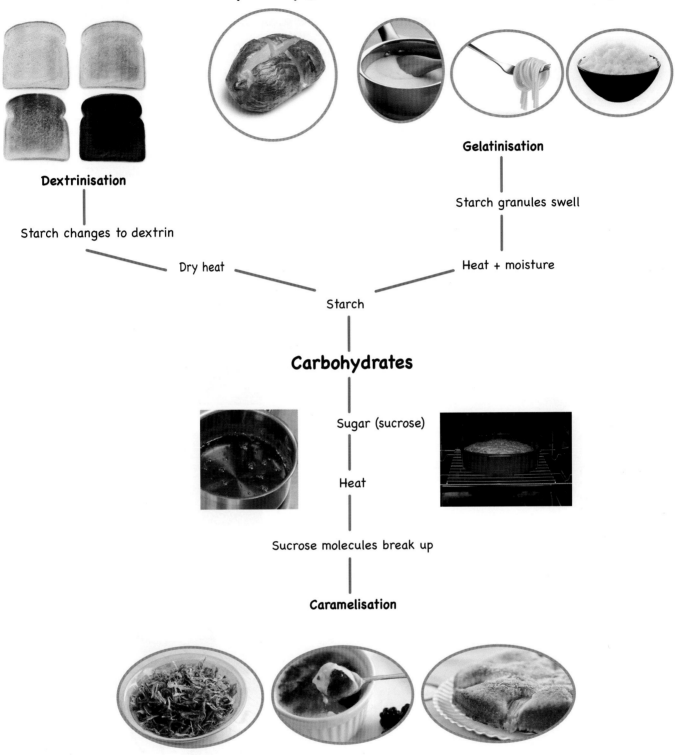

Dextrinisation

Starch changes to dextrin

Dry heat

Gelatinisation

Starch granules swell

Heat + moisture

Starch

Carbohydrates

Sugar (sucrose)

Heat

Sucrose molecules break up

Caramelisation

Revision tip

The mind map continues the key points.

Add to the revision map to include: explanations of the process, key temperatures, examples, etc.

Functional and chemical properties of food

What you must know about the food science of fats and oils

In your answers, you need to know how to explain the food science involved (the functional and chemical properties of fats and oils)

Further information you can add to extend your answers:

The **chemical structure** of fats and oils

- Fats are solid at room temperature
- Oils are fats that are liquid at room temperature

- Fats and oils have the same chemical structure:

glycerol — Fatty acid 1 / Fatty acid 2 / Fatty acid 3

The **plasticity** of fats

- Fats have **plasticity** – they can be spread and shaped

1. Chilled butter is very hard and difficult to spread – it has little plasticity

2. Butter at room temperature is softer and more plastic and can be spread easily

3. If it is heated, butter will melt to become an oil

- Plasticity is due to the **fatty acids**, which have different melting temperatures
- Fats with a lot of saturated fatty acids are harder and have less plasticity
- Fats with a lot of unsaturated fatty acids are softer and have more plasticity

The ability of fats to **'shorten'** a dough

Shortening

Fats are **rubbed-in** to flour to make:

- Short crust pastry
- Shortbread biscuits
- Cakes, e.g. rock cakes
- Crumble toppings
- Scones
- The most suitable fats for rubbing-in are: butter, solid (block) vegetable fat spread, lard and white vegetable fat spread
- The fat coats the flour particles with a waterproof layer
- When water is added, the gluten strands can only form short lengths because of the waterproof fat

- The texture of the pastry is 'short' and tender – not stretchy because of the short gluten molecules

waterproof fat layer / flour particle

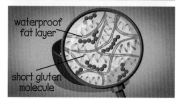

waterproof fat layer / short gluten molecule

The ability of fats to **aerate** a mixture	Aeration • Fats are used to **trap air** with sugar in cakes and other baked products • The process of beating fat and sugar together to trap air is called **creaming**	• Butter and vegetable fat spreads can **trap air** when beaten with sugar because they have **plasticity** • The trapped **air bubbles expand** when baking products such as cakes and give it a light texture
Emulsification of oil and water	Emulsification • Oil and water will not mix – they will **separate** if shaken together, e.g. in a salad dressing   • Oil and water can be made to mix together by using an **emulsifier** such as **lecithin** in egg yolk • Mayonnaise, Hollandaise sauce, milk, and butter are all **emulsions** 	• **Emulsifier molecules** have one end that **likes water (hydrophilic)** and one end that **doesn't like water (hydrophobic)** 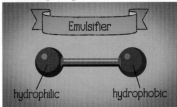 • When mixed into oil and water (e.g. in mayonnaise/Hollandaise sauce) the emulsifier molecules arrange themselves to prevent the oil and water from separating • This forms an emulsion of either: oil-in-water, or water-in-oil  

Applying your learning

You are piping some buttercream frosting onto some cupcakes.

1. Explain why it is best if the butter is at room temperature when you make the frosting.

2. Explain the food science behind how the butter makes it possible for the frosting to be piped into decorative shapes on the cakes.

Key terms you should try to use in your answers

Plasticity: the ability of a fat to soften over a range of temperatures and be shaped and spread with light pressure

Shortening: the ability of fats to shorten the length of gluten molecules in pastry

Aeration: the ability of some fats to trap lots of air bubbles when beaten together with sugar

Emulsification: either, keeping drops of oil or fat suspended in a liquid and preventing them from separating out; or keeping drops of water suspended in an oil or fat and preventing them from separating out

Applying your learning

You are making some shortcrust pastry for a quiche flan.

1. Explain why you should keep the ingredients cool when making the pastry.

2. Explain why the pastry will not be stretchy like bread dough.

3. Explain which type of flour should be used for the pastry and why.

4. Explain which type of fat should be used to make the pastry and why.

Here is a revision mind map to help you learn about the science of fats and oils

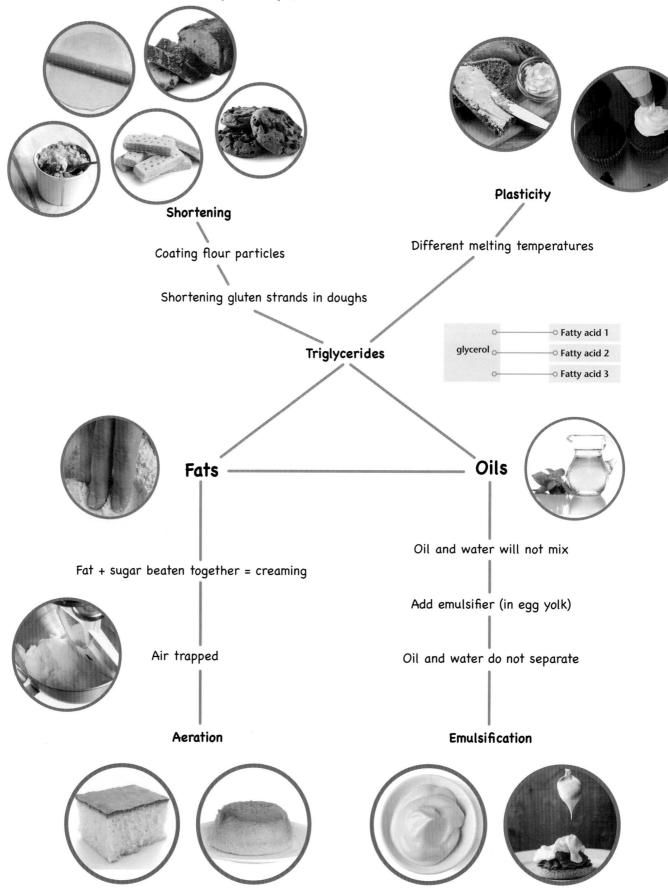

Shortening

Coating flour particles

Shortening gluten strands in doughs

Plasticity

Different melting temperatures

Triglycerides

glycerol	Fatty acid 1
	Fatty acid 2
	Fatty acid 3

Fats — **Oils**

Fat + sugar beaten together = creaming

Air trapped

Aeration

Oil and water will not mix

Add emulsifier (in egg yolk)

Oil and water do not separate

Emulsification

4 Raising agents

Book-link:
2.2.4 Raising agents, pages 140–154

What you must know about the food science of raising agents

In your answers, you need to know how to explain the food science involved (the functional and chemical properties of raising agents)

Further information you can add to extend your answers:

What a raising agent is

A raising agent is something that is added to baked mixtures to introduce gas bubbles that will expand when they are cooked and make the baked mixture rise:

Raising agents can be classified into three groups according to how they are introduced into a mixture:

Mechanical, e.g.:

- Sieving **air** into flour

- Folding puff pastry and trapping **air**

- Whisking eggs and sugar to trap **air**

- Beating/creaming fat and sugar together to trap **air**

- Rubbing fat into flour to trap **air**

- Adding water to turn to **steam**, **e.g.** in Yorkshire puddings, choux pastry

Chemical, e.g.:

- Adding baking powder or bicarbonate of soda to produce **carbon dioxide (CO_2) gas**

Biological, e.g.:

- Adding yeast to produce **CO_2 gas**

Types of raising agent: **Air** 	Air is a mixture of gases • Air is added to mixtures by sieving flour; whisking eggs and sugar; beating (creaming) fat and sugar; rolling and folding pastry dough; rubbing fat into flour	Air can be easily lost from mixtures, so care needs to be taken when adding other ingredients, e.g.: • When making a whisked sponge, flour must be carefully folded into the whisked egg and sugar mixture to avoid bursting the air bubbles
Types of raising agent: Carbon dioxide	• CO_2 gas is produced by baking powder (bicarbonate of soda + cream of tartar) • It is also produced by yeast (see below) • The bubbles of CO_2 gas expand when the mixture is baked • Self-raising (SR) flour has baking powder already added in the correct ratio	• If bicarbonate of soda (an **alkali**) is used on its own in a mixture, it will produce lots of CO_2 gas, but the chemical reaction involved will leave an inedible soapy taste in the baked mixture • This is only suitable for strongly flavoured mixtures, e.g. gingerbread • To avoid this in other mixtures such as scones, an **acid** is added (cream of tartar), which neutralises the reaction so that it tastes normal
Types of raising agent: Yeast 	• Used in bread making • When bread is baked, the CO_2 gas expands and raises the dough • Yeast will only work very slowly if it is too cold • Yeast is destroyed by boiling water, and salt • **Food (sugar/starch), warmth, water** and **time** • This process is called **fermentation**	• Yeast is a **microscopic plant** that produces CO_2 gas and alcohol when given these conditions • The alcohol evaporates in the heat of the oven during baking
Types of raising agent: Steam 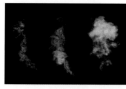	• Steam is produced when water is heated to a high temperature • Steam will cause a mixture to expand and rise	• The oven must be **very hot** for steam to be produced • The oven door should not be opened during the baking time as the mixture will not have set and the steam will escape

Key terms you should try to use in your answers

Raising agent: an ingredient or process that introduces a gas into a mixture so that it rises when cooked

Aerate: to mix (incorporate) air into a mixture

Revision tip

Raising agents can only work if the mixture they are added to is made correctly, so when you are revising this topic and answering a question about it, remember to show your understanding of the importance of other ingredients in baked mixtures, e.g.:

• In order for bread to be able to rise, the dough must have enough gluten and water to make it stretchy so that the gas bubbles produced by the yeast can expand.

• When making a whisked sponge cake (e.g. Swiss roll), it is important that the eggs and sugar are whisked until the mixture leaves a visible trail for at least 5 seconds so that there is enough air in the mixture to make it rise.

Applying your learning

You are making some profiteroles (choux pastry), and will bake them in a gas oven.

1. Explain why you will need to bake the profiteroles on a shelf near the top of the gas oven and not on a low shelf.

2. Explain why using strong plain bread flour rather than ordinary plain flour for the choux pastry will help the profiteroles to rise well.

3. Why is choux pastry made in a saucepan?

4. What is the reason for beating the eggs into the paste?

Activity 4.2

To help you apply what you know about the food science of proteins, carbohydrates, fats and raising agents, choose a variety of recipes you have made and make notes alongside the method for each about the function of the ingredients used and the food science involved at each stage. Here is an example (showing some of the points in the method) and another on the next page for you to complete:

Recipe: Fishcakes

Stage in the method for making the recipe	What the ingredients do in the recipe (their functional properties)	The food science involved (their chemical properties)	Key food science terms involved
1. Peel the potatoes and cut into 1cm dice. 2. Place potatoes in a large pan, cover with cold water and bring to the boil. Simmer for 20 minutes until the potatoes are soft. 5. When the potatoes are cooked, drain and mash them until smooth.	Potatoes • When cooked and mashed, they help to hold all the other ingredients together • They allow the fishcakes to be shaped	• Potatoes contain starch in small packets (granules) • As they are cooking, the boiling water is soaked up (absorbed) by the starch • The starch granules swell up and eventually burst • The texture of the potato becomes soft	Gelatinisation
7. Crack the egg into a small bowl and beat with a fork. 10. Dip each fishcake into the egg mixture, brushing with a pastry brush.	Eggs • Allow the bread crumbs to stick to the fishcakes • Help to form a protective coating on the outside of the baked or fried fishcakes to protect the ingredients inside from being overcooked	• Eggs contain protein. • When heated, protein molecules denature as the chemical bonds holding them together break and then join up with other denatured protein molecules and coagulate (become solid and set) • Coagulation prevents the breadcrumbs from falling off the fishcakes	Chemical bonds Denaturation Coagulation
12. Bake the fishcakes in the hot oven on a greased baking tray for 15–20 minutes until golden brown and crispy on the outside. Or Shallow fry the fishcakes in a little hot oil until golden and crispy on both sides.	Breadcrumbs • Give a protective coating to the fishcakes so that the ingredients inside are not overcooked • Give a crunchy texture to the fishcakes	• The dry heat of the oven changes the starch to dextrin, which causes the colour change to golden brown • The heat of the oven drives water out of the breadcrumbs and makes them crispy	Dextrinisation

Activity 4.2 continued

Now have a go at completing the table for the method for making All-in-one chocolate and orange cake on page 128–129 in student book:

Stage in the method for making the recipe	What the ingredients do in the recipe (their functional properties)	The food science involved (their chemical properties)	Key food science terms involved
1. Basic cake mix – place all the ingredients for the basic cake mix (self raising flour, cocoa powder, baking powder, butter or vegetable fat spread, caster sugar, eggs, milk, orange zest) into a mixing bowl and whisk at medium speed with an electric whisk, or beat well with a wooden spoon until well mixed and light in texture and colour.			
3. Spread the mixture out evenly using a palette knife or the back of a spoon.			
4. Bake at 190°C, (180°C for fan ovens)/gas 4, for 20–25 minutes until the cakes are well risen and spongy to the touch.			
6. Frosting: Whisk or beat together the sieved icing sugar, cocoa and softened butter or vegetable fat spread until well mixed – it may be a bit dry at this stage, but that is quite normal. Add the orange juice, a teaspoonful at a time, until the mixture is smooth, creamy and easy to spread.			
8. Spread more frosting on the top of the cake and if you have enough left, you can then pipe it onto the top of the cake with a star nozzle and piping bag to decorate.			

Functional and chemical properties of food

Activity 4.3

To help you to think of examples, make a list of recipes you have made that include these functional and chemical properties of ingredients.

Recipes you have made that include these functional and chemical properties

Proteins

Protein denaturation

Protein coagulation

Gluten formation

Foam formation

Carbohydrates

Gelatinisation

Dextrinisation

Caramelisation

Recipes you have made that include these functional and chemical properties

Fats

Plasticity

Emulsification

Aeration

Shortening

Raising agents

Air

Carbon dioxide

Steam

Multiple choice challenge

Have a go at answering these questions. They are worth **one mark** each. Answers are on page 145.

1. **Protein molecules are made up units called:**
   - a) Acetic acids
   - b) Amino acids
   - c) Fatty acids
   - d) Citric acids

2. **Protein can be denatured by:**
   - a) Whisking eggs and sugar together
   - b) Heating food
   - c) Adding lemon juice to raw meat in a marinade
   - d) All of these

3. **Gluten is a protein which allows bread dough to:**
   - a) Stretch, rise and expand
   - b) Soften, rise and expand
   - c) Stretch, rise and gelatinise
   - d) Solidify, shrink and expand

4. **Starch granules start to swell up in water when it reaches:**
   - a) 100°C
   - b) 80°C
   - c) 60°C
   - d) 50°C

5. **The name of the process when starch granules swell and thicken a sauce is called:**
   - a) Gelatinisation
   - b) Dextrinisation
   - c) Caramelisation
   - d) Shortening

6. **The name of the process when dry heat causes the starch in bread to become toast is:**
   - a) Gelatinisation
   - b) Dextrinisation
   - c) Caramelisation
   - d) Shortening

7. **The name of the process when fat shortens gluten strands in pastry making is:**
   - a) Gelatinisation
   - b) Dextrinisation
   - c) Caramelisation
   - d) Shortening

8. **The name of the process when boiling sugar causes it to change to a golden brown colour is:**
   - a) Gelatinisation
   - b) Dextrinisation
   - c) Caramelisation
   - d) Shortening

9. **The name of the process when fat and sugar are beaten together to trap air is:**
   - a) Plasticity
   - b) Creaming
   - c) Emulsification
   - d) Shortening

10. **The name of the process when oil and water are prevented from separating from each other is:**
    - a) Plasticity
    - b) Creaming
    - c) Emulsification
    - d) Shortening

11. **The name of the process when fat is able to be spread and shaped is:**
    - a) Plasticity
    - b) Creaming
    - c) Emulsification
    - d) Shortening

12. **The name of the emulsifier found in egg yolk is:**
    - a) Mayonnaise
    - b) Vitamin D
    - c) Iron
    - d) Lecithin

13. **Air can be trapped in a mixture by:**
    - a) Whisking eggs
    - b) Sieving flour
    - c) Creaming fat and sugar
    - d) All of these

14. **Which is the main raising agent used when making bread?**
    - a) Bicarbonate of soda
    - b) Yeast
    - c) Steam
    - d) Air

15. **Which is the main raising agent used when making choux pastry?**
    - a) Bicarbonate of soda
    - b) Yeast
    - c) Steam
    - d) Air

16. **Which is the main raising agent used when making scones?**
    - a) Bicarbonate of soda
    - b) Yeast
    - c) Steam
    - d) Air

17. **Which is the main raising agent used when making a Swiss roll?**
    - a) Bicarbonate of soda
    - b) Yeast
    - c) Steam
    - d) Air

18. **Which conditions does yeast need to make it work?**
    - a) Warmth, moisture, salt and time
    - b) Warmth, moisture, sugar or starch and time
    - c) Warmth, moisture, sugar or starch and time
    - d) Cold, moisture, sugar or starch and time

19. **The process where yeast makes CO_2 gas to make bread rise is called:**
    - a) Gelatinisation
    - b) Foam formation
    - c) Fermentation
    - d) Denaturation

20. **What is the name of the gas produced by yeast and bicarbonate of soda?**
    - a) Carbon monoxide
    - b) Carbon dioxide
    - c) Oxygen
    - d) Nitrogen

Knowledge check – can you recall...?

(Answers on pages 148–149)

1. The chemical structure of protein molecules? *(2 marks)*
2. What the word 'denaturation' means? *(1 mark)*
3. What the word 'coagulation' means? *(1 mark)*
4. Three reasons why gluten is important in baked products? *(3 marks)*
5. How foams are formed using egg whites? *(2 marks)*
6. What happens to starch when it is heated with a liquid? *(4 marks)*
7. What happens to starch when it is heated under a grill or in an oven? *(2 marks)*
8. What caramelisation means? *(1 mark)*
9. What gelatinisation means? *(1 mark)*
10. What dextrinisation means? *(1 mark)*
11. The chemical structure of fat molecules? *(2 marks)*
12. What plasticity means? *(1 mark)*
13. What shortening means? *(1 mark)*
14. How fats aerate a mixture? *(2 marks)*
15. How oil and water are emulsified? *(3 marks)*
16. Four ways in which air can be trapped in a mixture? *(4 marks)*
17. Two ways in which carbon dioxide gas can be introduced into a mixture? *(2 marks)*
18. How gases from raising agents make a baked mixture rise? *(2 marks)*
19. The four conditions yeast needs to be able to produce carbon dioxide gas? *(4 marks)*
20. Why the oven must be very hot in order for batters (e.g. Yorkshire puddings) and choux pastry to rise? *(2 marks)*

Stretch and challenge questions

1. Using your knowledge of the functional and chemical properties of foods, explain what are the possible causes of each of the following:

   a) You have made some baked egg custards in the oven, but when you serve them their texture is watery and tough. *(2 marks)*

   b) You have made some bread and it has a very dense texture and has not risen very much. *(3 marks)*

   c) You have made a béchamel sauce to go with some pasta, but the sauce is lumpy. *(2 marks)*

2. Explain, with details and examples, the reasons for the following instructions in these recipes:

   a) Yorkshire puddings: Pre-heat the oven until it is very hot (gas 7/220°C). *(2 marks)*

   b) Swiss roll: Sieve the flour twice and fold it very carefully into the egg and sugar mixture, using a metal spoon. *(2 marks)*

   c) Shortcrust pastry: Rub the fat into the flour with the fingertips, until the mixture looks like breadcrumbs. *(2 marks)*

   d) Crème caramel: Boil the sugar in the pan until a golden brown colour. Remove from the heat straightaway and pour into the ramekin dishes. Do not leave the pan on the heat. *(2 marks)*

3. 3. Explain, giving details and examples, the reason(s) for the following:

   a) Properly made mayonnaise does not separate into oil and water. *(3 marks)*

   b) Scones made with bicarbonate of soda as the only raising agent taste soapy. *(3 marks)*

   c) Ganache, made with chocolate melted into warmed cream, can be used to pipe decorations on cakes and desserts if it is cooled to the right temperature. *(3 marks)*

4. Explain the functional and chemical properties of the following ingredients in the recipes shown:

   a) Flour in bread making. *(3 marks)*

   a) Eggs in a whisked sponge mixture. (e.g. Swiss roll) *(3 marks)*

   b) Water and eggs in choux pastry. *(3 marks)*

   c) Flour in a béchamel sauce. *(3 marks)*

Chapter 5: Food spoilage and contamination

1 **Micro-organisms and enzymes**

Book-link:
3.1.1 Micro-organisms and enzymes, pages 158–160

Micro-organisms (Microbes) and Enzymes can cause food spoilage and make food unsafe and unfit to eat.

Key learning: Micro-organisms

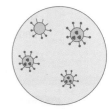

What micro-organisms are	They are: • Tiny plants and animals • Often called microbes	They are so small; you can only see them under a microscope.
What they are called	• Bacteria • Moulds • Yeasts	There are many different types of each.
Where they come from	Many places: Air, water, soil, dust, dirt, sewage, food, food packaging, clothing, rubbish, surfaces, equipment, people, insects, animals, birds	They are so small that it is usually impossible to know they are there.
What they do to food	They live on or in food where they grow and multiply	If food is stored, handled, prepared and cooked properly, it is possible to slow down or prevent them from multiplying.

What makes them grow and multiply	They need the following conditions to be right so they can grow and multiply quickly:
	
	• The right temperature
	• Enough moisture
	• Food to eat
	• Time to grow
	• The right amount of acid or alkali (pH)

		• Cooking food to a high temperature (at least 75°C) will kill many microbes.
		• If food is cooled to a low temperature (e.g. 0–5°C in a refrigerator) microbes will still grow and multiply, but only very slowly.
		• If the temperature becomes very cold (e.g. –18°C in a freezer), microbes become inactive (dormant) but are still alive.
		• Removing moisture from food will kill many microbes.
		• Covering food and storing it correctly will stop microbes coming into contact with it.
		• Some microbes are killed by:
		  – acids e.g. vinegar in pickles
		  – high levels of salt, e.g. dried salted fish, or sugar e.g. jam

Why they make food unsafe and unfit to eat	• They put waste products and poisons into the food. • If people eat these, they can be very ill with food poisoning. • Large numbers of microbes in a food can make people ill because they irritate the digestive system.	• Not all microbes make people ill. • Some microbes are needed for food production, e.g. bacteria to make yogurt. • Microbes that do make people ill are called **pathogenic** (harmful) **microbes**.

Key terms you should try to use in your answers

Micro-organisms: tiny plants and animals; only visible under a microscope

Contaminate: making a food unsafe to eat by allowing it to come into contact with micro-organisms that will grow and multiply in it

Food poisoning: an illness caused by pathogenic micro-organisms which have contaminated some food, e.g. Salmonella in undercooked chicken

Pathogenic: something that is capable of causing illness in people

High-risk foods: foods that contain a lot of moisture and nutrients such as protein (e.g. milk, cream, eggs, meat, fish), and easily allow pathogenic micro-organisms to grow and multiply, particularly bacteria. Also called perishable foods.

Revision tip

You must be able to show that you kn about the three main types of micro-organisms and how you can prevent t from causing food spoilage and food poisoning when you are preparing and cooking food.

ACTIVITY 5.1

Look at these foods:

1. Describe what you can see in each of the three pictures above. *(3 marks)*

2. What might happen to a person if they ate these foods? *(2 marks)*

3. Why do the foods look like this? Evaluate and explain what has happened to them. *(3 marks)*

Applying your learning

You have been food shopping.

Explain how and where you would store fresh bread, apples and fresh meat at home to prevent them from spoiling and becoming unsafe and unfit to eat.

2 The signs of food spoilage

Book-link:
3.1.1 Micro-organisms and enzymes, page 160
3.1.2 The signs of food spoilage, pages 161–164

How enzymes change and spoil food

What you must know about enzymes

In your answers, you need to know how to explain:

Further information you can add to extend your answers:

What enzymes are	Natural substances found in foods and living plants and animals	They are usually proteins
Where they come from	They are found inside the cells of plants and animals 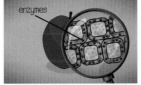	Enzymes are released when an animal dies or plant cells are broken open by cutting and bruising 
What they do to food	• Ripen fruits and vegetables • Make unripe fruits change colour and become softer, juicier and sweeter • Break down the tissues of dead animals and fish	• **Ripening** changes the colour, flavour and texture of fruits and vegetables • Meat is tenderised
What makes them work	• The right temperature • Oxygen from the air • The right level of acidity (pH)	• Cooking destroys **enzymes** and stops them working • Preventing foods from mixing with the air (oxygen) prevents them from working • Adding acids (e.g. lemon juice) to foods destroys the enzymes and stops them working
Why they change food and can make it unfit to eat	• Fruits and vegetables can become over-ripe, which makes them too soft and mushy • Some fruits and vegetables become discoloured (brown/black) when cut and open to the air • Discoloured fruits and vegetables are safe to eat but do not look appetising (you don't want to eat them)	• Some fruits are bought under-ripe and take a few days to ripen at home, e.g. bananas • Over-ripe fruit and vegetables will quickly go mouldy, e.g. strawberries • To prevent browning of fruits and vegetables either cook them, cover them in water (to keep out the air) or add acid (lemon juice)

Key terms you should try to use in your answers

Food spoilage: means something happens which makes food unfit and unsafe to eat

Enzymes: natural substances in plants and animals that speed up chemical reactions

Catalyst: a substance that speeds up the rate of a chemical reaction

Ripening: the process of a fruit or vegetable maturing so that it is ready to eat

Enzymic browning: the discolouration of a fruit or vegetable due to the reaction of enzymes with plant cell substances and oxygen from the air

Revision tip

Make sure that you can explain and give examples of how enzymes can be prevented from causing food spoilage.

ACTIVITY 5·2

A   B   C

Look at these foods:

1. Describe what you can see in each of the three pictures above. *(3 marks)*

2. Why do the foods look like this?
   Evaluate and explain what has happened to them. *(3 marks)*

3. Will it be safe to eat them? Give reasons for your answer. *(2 marks)*

Applying your learning

You are making a fruit salad.

What can you do to prevent some of the fruits from turning brown and spoiling the look of the fruit salad?

Explain how this would work.

How moulds spoil foods

What you must know about moulds	In your answers, you need to know how to explain:	Further information you can add to extend your answers:
What moulds are and where they come from	They are: • Tiny plants • They send out tiny **spores** into the air which settle on food	• There are lots of different types of moulds • They are related to mushrooms
What they do to food to make it unsafe and unfit to eat	• Moulds send out tiny spores which land on the surface of food • If conditions are right, spores germinate and send down roots into the food and you can see the mould growing on the surface of the food • The waste products from the mould go into the food and can cause food poisoning	• It is possible to see moulds growing on food • They make the food taste and smell very unpleasant • The waste products they produce contain **poisons** (**toxins**) that can make people ill • The waste products can stay in the food even if the visible mould is cut off  
What makes them grow and multiply	The right conditions: • Warm temperatures • Moisture • Food • The right amount of acidity • Time	• Moulds will grow slowly in cold conditions (refrigerators) • Moulds will grow where there is a lot of moisture, e.g. inside an air tight plastic food box or a poorly ventilated cupboard (no fresh air)

How yeasts spoil foods

What you must know about yeasts	In your answers, you need to know how to explain:		Further information you can add to extend your answers:
What yeasts are and where they come from	They are: • Tiny plants • Wild yeasts are found in the air and will settle on a variety of foods, e.g. fruit, flour and water batter		• Wild yeasts are used to make sour dough bread
What they do to food to make it unsafe and unfit to eat	• They **ferment** (break down) sugars into CO_2 gas and alcohol		• Lots of pale brown spots will appear on the surface of the food • Fermentation by yeasts can happen in processed foods such as fruit yogurts, dried fruits and fruit juices
What makes them grow and multiply	• Sugars in food • Temperature – ideally 25°C–37°C • Moisture • Time		• Yeasts multiply by 'budding'

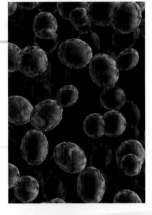

THEORY INTO PRACTICE
– try this practical challenge

- Make a batch of bread dough using either fresh or dried yeast. You could use the bread roll recipe in the student book on page 112.
- Knead the dough and then divide it in half.
- Place each half of the dough into a separate mixing bowl and cover each with cling film.
- Place one bowl (dough A) in a warm place and leave it for at least one hour.
- Place the other bowl (dough B) in the refrigerator.
- After one hour, compare how much the two doughs have risen.
- Place dough B back in the refrigerator and leave it in there overnight.
- Shape dough A into rolls and bake them.
- The next morning, look at dough B and answer the following questions. You can then use dough B to make some more bread rolls.

QUESTIONS

Using your knowledge of the conditions that micro-organisms need to grow and multiply, answer these questions:

- After one hour, which dough has risen the most? Explain why. *(2 marks)*
- Explain what has happened to the yeast in dough B after a night in the refrigerator. What does this tell you about the effects of temperature on the activity of yeast? *(2 marks)*
- If you wanted to make some fresh home-made bread for breakfast, what could you do to save time in the morning? *(1 mark)*

Book-link: see p112 for a recipe

Key terms you should try to use in your answers

Spores: the name for the 'seeds' which moulds send out so they can spread to other foods

Toxin: another name for a poison, which is produced by micro-organisms and can make people ill with food poisoning

Fermentation: the name for the process where yeasts break down sugars and change them into CO_2 gas and alcohol

3 Micro-organisms in food production

Book-link:
3.1.3 Micro-organisms in food production, pages 165–170

Some micro-organisms **do not** cause food poisoning and are used to make different food products:
Micro-organisms used in food production

Bread	The micro-organism that is used: • Yeast – specially produced for baking	• Fresh, dried and fast-acting dried yeast is available • The yeast needs warmth, moisture, starch/sugar and time to ferment the starch and sugar to CO_2 gas and alcohol
Cheese 	The micro-organisms that are used: • Bacteria – specially produced in large amounts called a **culture** • Moulds – specially produced in controlled conditions	• Milk is **pasteurised** to kill pathogenic bacteria • **Non-pathogenic** (safe) bacteria and moulds are used in cheese making • Bacteria culture added to milk turns lactose in the milk into lactic acid • Lactic acid adds flavour, texture and preserves cheese • Rennet added – turns milk to curds (solid) and whey (liquid) • Whey drained off • Curds cut up, salt added, then curds are pressed • Bacteria ripen the cheese to develop flavour • Cheese left to mature for a few weeks • Blue cheeses have a safe mould added to produce blue veins and flavour
Yogurt 	• Bacteria	• Special bacteria culture added to pasteurised and **homogenised** milk • Milk held at 42 °C to let bacteria ferment the lactose sugar to lactic acid • The milk becomes semi-solid due to **coagulation** of protein by lactic acid • Milk cooled – flavouring may be added

Key terms you should try to use in your answers

Pasteurisation: this means heating fresh milk to 72°C for 15 seconds in order to kill pathogenic microorganisms that may be in it

Non-pathogenic: this is a micro-organism that is not harmful to humans and does not cause food poisoning

Homogenisation: forcing milk under high pressure through a fine sieve, in order to break up the fat into tiny droplets. This means that the droplets stay suspended in the milk and do not separate out into a layer of cream

Coagulation: the joining together of lots of denatured protein molecules (see pp58–59), which changes the appearance and texture of the food

Applying your learning

You are making some bread.

Explain why you have to:

- Add warm water and sugar to fresh and ordinary dried yeast and leave it for 10 minutes before you add it to the flour.
- Knead the dough.
- Leave the dough to rise.
- Bake the bread in a very hot oven.

4 Bacterial contamination

Book-link:
3.1.4 Bacterial contamination, pages 171–184

Bacteria and food poisoning

What you must know about bacteria and food poisoning	In your answers, you need to know how to explain:	Further information you can add to extend your answers:
What food poisoning is	• A common and unpleasant illness that can lead to serious health problems	• Bacteria cause the most cases of food poisoning • Food poisoning is especially dangerous for young children, pregnant women, elderly people and those people who have been ill or have a weak immune system
The symptoms of food poisoning	 • Bad stomach ache • Diarrhoea • Feeling sick (nausea) • Being sick (vomiting) • Headache • Dizziness • A high body temperature • Feeling cold and shivery	• A person with food poisoning is not likely to have all these symptoms • Different types of bacteria cause different symptoms • A person can start to feel ill anything from a few hours to a few days after they have eaten food contaminated with pathogenic bacteria • They may feel ill for several days
Why bacteria cause food poisoning	• Most bacteria cause it inside the **digestive system** (the stomach and intestines) • Some bacteria get into the bloodstream and go round the body causing damage to body organs, e.g. the liver and kidneys	• They are so small that they cannot be easily seen, smelt or tasted • They are found in so many different places that it is easy for them to get into food • They can easily be passed from one place (e.g. hands) into food by **cross-contamination**  • They can multiply very quickly in the right conditions

The most common bacteria that cause food poisoning	• Campylobacter • Escherichia Coli (E.Coli) • Salmonella • Listeria • Staphylococcus Aureus (S. Aureus)	• There are many more different types of pathogenic bacteria
Which foods they are found in	• **Campylobacter:** raw poultry and meat; milk; dirty water • **Escherichia Coli (E. Coli) :** meat, minced beef (e.g. undercooked burgers); untreated (raw) milk; dirty water • **Salmonella:** raw and undercooked poultry, eggs and meat; untreated (raw) milk • **Listeria:** soft cheeses; cheeses made from untreated (raw) milk; salads; pâtés • **Staphylococcus Aureus (S. Aureus):** untreated (raw) milk; cold cooked meats; dairy foods plus: • people – their hands, nose, mouth, throat, skin cuts and infections	• Young children, pregnant women, elderly people and those people who have been ill or have a weak immune system should avoid eating the following foods: • Raw and undercooked eggs, poultry and meat • Cheeses made from untreated (raw) milk • Unwashed salads • Pâtés • Untreated (raw) milk 
What makes them grow and multiply	The right conditions: • Warm temperatures • Moisture • Food • Time • Acidity Water boils 100°C → 100°C Bacteria cells are dead. Bacteria spores can survive very high temperatures Cook from raw to at least 75°C Re-heat cooked food only once to at least 75°C Bacteria start to die Keep cooked food hot above 63°C → The danger zone Bacteria multiply rapidly 5°C to 63°C Bacteria multiply slowly Chill food to 0°C to below 5°C → Freeze food to –18°C to –24°C → Bacteria do not multiply. They are dormant – alive but inactive	• Different temperatures affect how fast or slowly bacteria grow and multiply: • The **danger zone** (when they grow the most rapidly) is **5°C to 63°C** • Bacteria multiply every 20 minutes • Many millions will be produced in a few hours 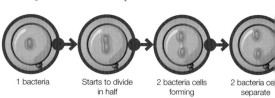 1 bacteria — Starts to divide in half — 2 bacteria cells forming — 2 bacteria cells separate
Why they make food unsafe and unfit to eat	• Bacteria produce waste products and poisons (toxins) which can make us ill • Large numbers of bacteria irritate our digestive system, which is what also makes us feel ill	• If conditions are not right bacteria produce **spores** • The bacteria stay inside the spore and when conditions are right they **germinate** • If bacteria spores germinate, they produce very strong and dangerous poisons (toxins), which can cause serious illness and even death

conditions too cold too dry no food

spores form around bacteria which remain alive but inactive

conditions just right / dangerous toxins (poisons) produced / spores germinate / bacteria becomes active

Here is a chart to help you remember the most common food poisoning bacteria:

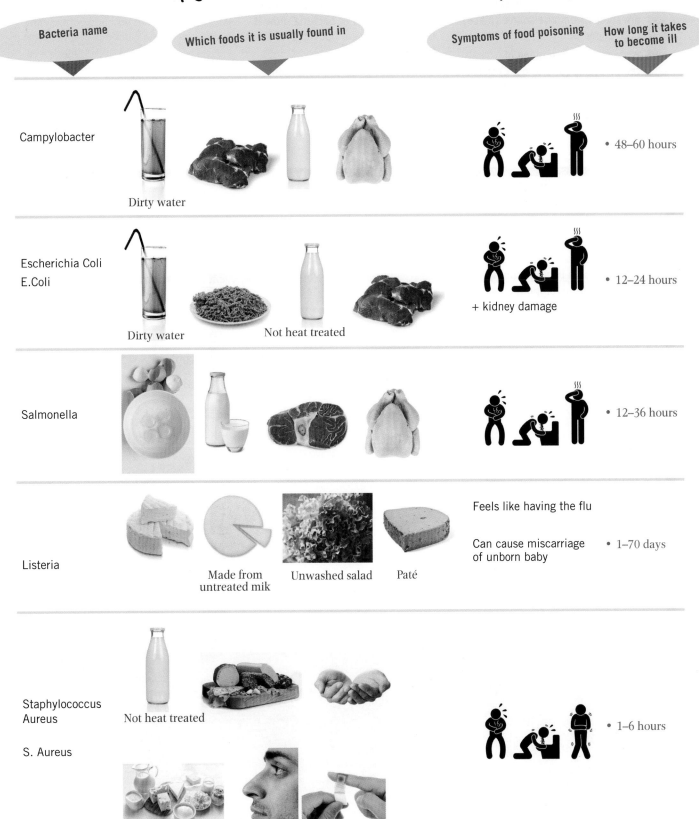

Bacteria name	Which foods it is usually found in	Symptoms of food poisoning	How long it takes to become ill
Campylobacter	Dirty water		• 48–60 hours
Escherichia Coli E.Coli	Dirty water · Not heat treated	+ kidney damage	• 12–24 hours
Salmonella			• 12–36 hours
Listeria	Made from untreated mik · Unwashed salad · Paté	Feels like having the flu · Can cause miscarriage of unborn baby	• 1–70 days
Staphylococcus Aureus / S. Aureus	Not heat treated		• 1–6 hours

Revision tip

In your answers, you will need to show that you understand how bacteria can be prevented from causing food poisoning by the correct handling, storage and cooking of food.

ACTIVITY 5.3

Label (annotate) the thermometer with each of the phrases given in the box:

- Danger zone: bacteria multiply rapidly between these temperatures
- Bacteria cells are dead: bacteria spores can survive these temperatures
- Bacteria do not multiply: they are dormant – alive but inactive at this temperature
- Bacteria multiply slowly at this temperature
- Bacteria start to die at this temperature
- Water boils at this temperature
- Chill food to this temperature
- Keep cooked food hot at this temperature
- Freeze food to this temperature
- Cook food from raw to at least this temperature
- Re-heat cooked food only once to at least this temperature

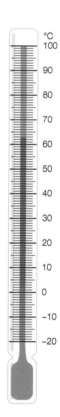

°C
100
90
80
70
60
50
40
30
20
10
0
−10
−20

Applying your learning

When you are preparing food, which coloured chopping board should you use for each of the following foods?

Raw fish _____

Root vegetables _____

Cooked meat, fish and poultry _____

Bakery and dairy foods _____

Salads, leaves and fruits _____

Raw meat and poultry _____

ACTIVITY 5.4

Fill in the table below:

How to prevent cross-contamination of micro-organisms when you are handling food:	Explain why each is necessary and important (2 marks each):
1. Wear clean clothing; tie long hair back; have clean, short finger nails; don't wear jewellery or nail polish.	1.
2. Wash your hands before, during and after handling food; after using the toilet; after handling rubbish.	2.
3. Do not cough or sneeze over food.	3.
4. Do not lick fingers or a spoon and put them back into food.	4.
5. Separate raw foods from cooked food during storage and preparation.	5.
6. Store food correctly at the right temperature.	6.
7. Check that the refrigerator/freezer temperatures are correct.	7.
8. Check the use-by dates on high risk foods.	8.
9. Check the quality and freshness of fresh foods such as meat and fish.	9.
10. Check that food packaging is not damaged.	10.
11. Make sure food is cooked right through to at least 75°C.	11.
12. Use coloured chopping boards for different foods.	12.
13. Thoroughly wash, rinse and dry equipment used to store, prepare and serve food.	13.
14. Cover any cuts/sores on your hands and arms.	14.
15. Protect food from dust and pests – insects, animals, and birds.	15.
16. Get rid of rubbish regularly and away from the food preparation area.	16.

Multiple choice challenge

Have a go at answering these questions. They are worth **one mark** each. Answers are on page 145.

1. **For bacteria to grow and multiply rapidly they need the following conditions:**
   - a) Warmth, moisture, air, pH and food
   - b) Food, moisture, warmth, time and light
   - c) Moisture, warmth, pH, food and time
   - d) Time, moisture, pH, light and warmth

2. **There are three groups of micro-organisms:**
   - a) Bacteria, moulds and algae
   - b) Yeasts, bacteria and spores
   - c) Spores, bacteria and moulds
   - d) Bacteria, yeasts and moulds

3. **Micro-organisms that cause food poisoning are known as:**
   - a) Homogenised
   - b) Pathogenic
   - c) Emulsified
   - d) Pathetic

4. **Cooling food to a very low temperature will make the growth of microbes slow right down until they are:**
   - a) Destroyed
   - b) Dehydrated
   - c) Denatured
   - d) Dormant

5. **High-risk foods allow harmful micro-organisms to grow and multiply because they:**
   - a) Contain a lot of moisture and protein
   - b) Contain a lot of sugar
   - c) Contain a lot of preservatives
   - d) Contain a lot of air

6. **When micro-organisms come into contact with food and make it unsafe to eat, the food is said to be:**
   - a) Conserved
   - b) Contaminated
   - c) Concentrated
   - d) Condensed

7. **Green bananas gradually become yellow in colour, softer in texture and sweeter in flavour. This is due to:**
   - a) Ripening caused by bacteria
   - b) Mould growth
   - c) The action of enzymes
   - d) The action of sunlight

8. **Cut fruits and vegetables can be prevented from discolouring by:**
   - a) Cooking them
   - b) Adding lemon juice to them
   - c) Covering them in water until ready to be served
   - d) All of these

9. **These are produced by moulds to enable them to multiply:**
   - a) Spores
   - b) Stalks
   - c) Sprouts
   - d) Shells

10. **How should cheddar cheese be stored to prevent it from becoming mouldy?**
    - a) In an air tight box in a kitchen cupboard
    - b) In an air tight box on the kitchen worktop
    - c) Wrapped in plastic cling film in a kitchen cupboard
    - d) In an air tight box in a refrigerator

11. **Yeasts cause food to ferment, which means that:**
    - a) Sugars are changed into CO_2 gas and alcohol
    - b) Fats are turned into CO_2 gas and alcohol
    - c) Sugars are changed into O_2 and alcohol
    - d) Proteins are turned into O_2 and alcohol

12. **To make yogurt, a special bacteria culture is added to milk.**
    - a) The bacteria produce carbon dioxide which makes the milk set
    - b) The bacteria produce lactic acid which makes the milk set
    - c) The bacteria produce bicarbonate of soda which makes the milk set

Knowledge check – can you recall...?
(Answers on page 149)

1. What food spoilage means? *(1 mark)*
2. What enzymes are? *(1 mark)*
3. The names of the three types of micro-organisms? *(3 marks)*
4. Five places where you find micro-organisms? *(5 marks)*
5. The five conditions micro-organisms need to grow and multiply? *(5 marks)*
6. What happens to micro-organisms if the temperature is very cold? *(1 mark)*
7. What happens to micro-organisms if the temperature is very hot? *(1 mark)*
8. The names of the five main types of bacteria that cause food poisoning? *(5 marks)*
9. What pathogenic means? *(1 mark)*
10. What high risk foods are and give three examples of them? *(4 marks)*
11. What the Danger zone is? *(1 mark)*
12. Why bacteria spores are particularly dangerous? *(1 mark)*
13. The four groups of people who should avoid eating high-risk foods such as soft cheeses and undercooked meat and eggs? *(4 marks)*
14. Why it is not a good idea to scrape mould off a food and then eat the rest of the food? *(1 mark)*
15. Why do some vegetables and fruits turn brown after a few minutes when you cut them? *(1 mark)*
16. What fermentation means? *(1 mark)*
17. What pasteurisation means? *(1 mark)*
18. Why lactic acid produced by bacteria in yogurt making makes it change from a liquid to a semi-solid? *(1 mark)*
19. When making cheese, which two things milk turns into when rennet is added? *(2 marks)*
20. How enzymes change the colour, texture and flavour of unripe bananas? *(3 marks)*

Food spoilage and contamination

86

Stretch and challenge questions

1. In the UK, businesses such as restaurants and factories that produce food have to be regularly inspected by Environmental Health Officers to make sure that they are following the rules of the Food Safety Act.

    Evaluate why it is important that each of the following checks are made by Environmental Health Officers during one of these inspections. Give examples in your answers.

    a) Refrigerator and freezer temperatures. *(3 marks)*

    b) How food is stored in refrigerators and food cupboards. *(3 marks)*

    c) How food is handled by the staff during preparation. *(3 marks)*

    d) The disposal of waste and rubbish. *(3 marks)*

    e) The cleanliness of the kitchen, food store rooms, equipment and the staff toilet and hand washing facilities. *(3 marks)*

2. Giving details and examples, explain why the following are important in preventing food spoilage and food poisoning:

    a) Wearing clean, protective clothing when preparing food. *(3 marks)*

    b) Separating raw foods from cooked foods in a refrigerator. *(3 marks)*

    c) Regularly washing your hands when preparing and cooking food. *(3 marks)*

    d) Using different coloured chopping boards and different knives for different foods. *(3 marks)*

    e) Using a food probe when cooking meat or poultry. *(3 marks)*

3. Here are the stage-by-stage instructions for using a food probe when cooking.
    Analyse and evaluate why each stage is important from a food safety point of view, giving examples in your answer.

    (2 marks for each stage)

Reset the food probe before use

Stage 1

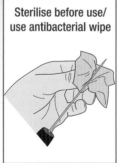

Sterilise before use/ use antibacterial wipe

Stage 2

Insert the probe into centre (core)/thickest part of the food

Stage 3

Do not touch the metal baking tin or pan base with the tip of the probe

Stage 4

Leave the probe in place until the temperature stabilises

Stage 5

The temperature must reach 75°C or above

Stage 6

The temperature must remain at 75°C or more for at least 2 minutes

2 min

Stage 7

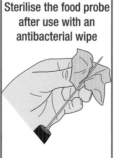

Sterilise the food probe after use with an antibacterial wipe

Stage 8

Chapter 6: Principles of food safety

1 | Buying and storing food

Book-link:
3.2.1 Buying and storing food, pages 185–192

What do you need to know?

You now know how and why foods can be spoiled and made unsafe to eat by micro-organisms.

Next you need to know:

- How to keep food **safe to eat** when you **buy, store, prepare, cook and serve** it
- How to prevent the **cross-contamination** of micro-organisms from one place then onto food
- Food **hygiene and safety rules** when preparing, cooking and serving food

Key learning: Buying food

What you must know about buying food	In your answers, you need to know how to explain:	Further information you can add to extend your answers:
Where food is bought	There are many different places where food can be bought: - Open air (street) and covered markets - Supermarkets - Independent shops, e.g. bakers, butchers - Farm shops - Online home delivery	- Most consumers have a choice of where to buy their food - Many consumers prefer to buy their food all in one place, e.g. a supermarket, to save time and effort - Online food shopping is popular and is useful for busy working people, people without transport, elderly and disabled people
What to look for when buying food	- Cleanliness of the shop/market - How well the food is displayed, e.g. is it priced clearly, easy to reach, labelled well; are raw foods kept separate from cooked foods? - Is the food packaging undamaged? If damaged, it could be a food safety risk - Is the food stored at the correct temperature, e.g. frozen foods below –18°C, chilled food 0°C to below 5°C - Food safety and hygiene practices of food handlers to avoid **cross-contamination**, e.g. do they use tongs or wear gloves when handling **high risk foods**, is their hair covered/tied back etc.? - The **use-by date** for high risk foods, e.g. meat, fish - The **best before date** for low risk foods, e.g. canned foods, biscuits, cereals etc.	- For online shopping, is the food delivered in good condition and at the right temperature for chilled/frozen food? - Is the delivery exactly what the consumer ordered, or has the supermarket used any substitute products, and if so, are they suitable? - Shops should rotate their food stocks so they sell the oldest foods first before they go out of date. 

What to look for when buying fresh fish		What to look for when buying fresh vegetables	
- Bright eyes, firm flesh and scales, moist skin, red gills, fresh smell		- Good colour, not wilted or damaged, no mould, firm and crisp, smooth skin, not too much soil	

What to look for when buying fresh meat		What to look for when buying fresh fruit	
- Not too much fat, firm moist flesh, good colour, fresh smell		- Good colour, not soft or damaged, no mould or yeast, firm and crisp, smooth skin	

Key terms you should try to use in your answers

Shelf-life: how long a food product will last before it becomes unsafe/unpalatable [unpleasant] to eat

Use-by date: the date by which high-risk/perishable foods should be eaten. After the use-by date food may not look or taste different, but it will be unsafe to eat

Best before/best before end (of month or year) date: after this date, a non-high-risk food will still be safe to eat, but not be at its best quality, e.g. have begun to go stale (changed in appearance, texture and flavour)

Ambient: ordinary room temperature; average between 19°C and 21°C, but variable according to the season

Tainted: when a food picks up the smell or flavour of another food nearby, which spoils its palatability

Food poisoning: an illness caused by pathogenic micro-organisms which have contaminated some food, e.g. salmonella

High-risk foods: foods that contain a lot of moisture and nutrients, e.g. protein

Applying your learning

You are going shopping for some vegetables (onions, parsnips, carrots, celery) to make a soup. The vegetables you buy come from local farms and are all different shapes and sizes.

Using your knowledge about the environmental impact and sustainability of food production, explain why it is important not to throw away and waste vegetables, just because they are not all the same shape and size.

Key learning: Food storage

What you must know about storing food	In your answers, you need to know how to explain:	Further information you can add to extend your answers:
Why food should be stored properly 	• To preserve its flavour, appearance, and nutritional value • To prevent food spoilage • To prevent the food becoming unsafe to eat • To prevent food wastage • Food must be stored at the correct temperature • It is important to avoid cross-contamination between different foods, e.g. cooked and raw meats	• Some foods need to be stored in the dark, e.g. potatoes, to prevent them developing a natural poison and turning green • It is important to prevent the smell of some foods, e.g. garlic, onion, strong cheese, from being transferred to (tainting) other foods
The different types of food storage: dry foods	Dry foods should be: • Stored at room temperature in a well-ventilated cupboard • Protected from pests (e.g. mice, rats, flies and other insects) and dust • Stored in air tight containers if they have been opened • Protected from moisture • Regularly checked to make sure they are not out of date	• If dry foods get wet, they may become mouldy and some go hard, e.g. icing sugar, flour • Some pests, e.g. mice, cockroaches, will eat dried foods and put urine and faeces into it so it becomes unfit to eat • Some pests, e.g. flies, will lay eggs in dried foods, which then hatch out into maggots and eat the food
The different types of food storage: refrigerated foods	Refrigerated foods should be: • Stored at 0°C to below 5°C (bacterial growth is slowed, but bacteria are still active at these temperatures) • Protected from moisture loss and taint (smells from other foods) • Fresh meat, poultry and fish should be stored in sealed containers on the bottom shelf to prevent them dripping on other foods	• High risk foods, e.g. fresh meat, fish and poultry, cream, milk, cheese, must be refrigerated • Do not overcrowd the refrigerator shelves because air will not circulate and chill the foods properly • Door seals should be checked to make sure they are working well and not letting warm air into the refrigerator

The different types of food storage: frozen foods	Frozen foods should be: • Stored at between –18°C and –24°C (bacteria become dormant [alive but not active] at these temperatures) • Protected from moisture loss and freezer burn – (food dries out and becomes discoloured) • Clearly labelled with the name of the food and date it was frozen – food is not always easy to identify once it is frozen	• Bacteria become active again in defrosted food • Frozen foods will gradually change colour, flavour and texture if stored for too long • The freezer should be regularly defrosted to make it work efficiently • The freezer door/lid seals should be checked to make sure they are working well • Some foods do not freeze well, e.g. cucumbers, lettuce, strawberries, because of their high water content
Materials for storing foods:	There are lots of types of packaging and storage materials and equipment available: • Plastic films, bags, and boxes • Greaseproof and silicon coated paper • Aluminium foil and dishes • Glass and ceramic (china) dishes	**Revision tip** Make sure that you know the correct storage temperatures for chilled and frozen foods. When answering questions about the importance of correct food storage, make sure you show your knowledge and understanding of the causes of food spoilage and contamination by micro-organisms, by giving examples where appropriate.

ACTIVITY 6·1

Draw lines to show on which shelf in the refrigerator you would store each of the foods shown below:

Give a reason for each of your answers.

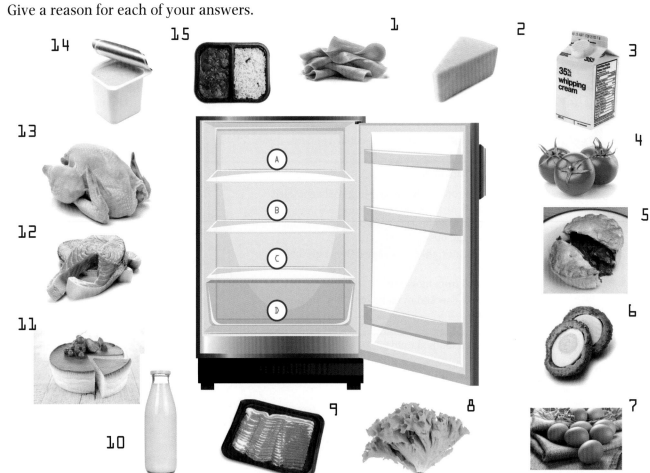

2 Food safety rules when preparing, cooking and serving food

Book-link: 3.2.2 Preparing, cooking and serving food, pages 192–201

Key learning: Preventing cross-contamination

The main source of cross-contamination (spreading bacteria from one place then onto food) is the people who handle food.

Personal hygiene when handling food is really important:

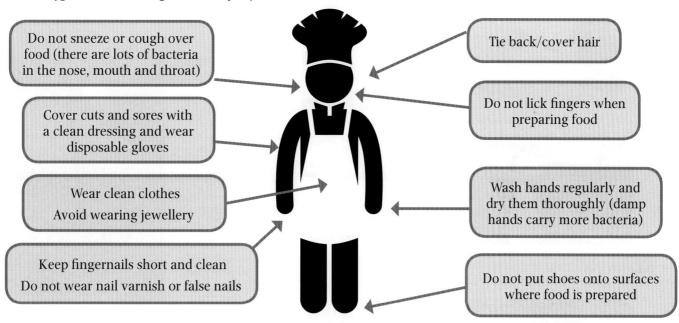

Do not sneeze or cough over food (there are lots of bacteria in the nose, mouth and throat)

Cover cuts and sores with a clean dressing and wear disposable gloves

Wear clean clothes
Avoid wearing jewellery

Keep fingernails short and clean
Do not wear nail varnish or false nails

Tie back/cover hair

Do not lick fingers when preparing food

Wash hands regularly and dry them thoroughly (damp hands carry more bacteria)

Do not put shoes onto surfaces where food is prepared

Food preparation rules should be followed to prevent cross-contamination of bacteria:

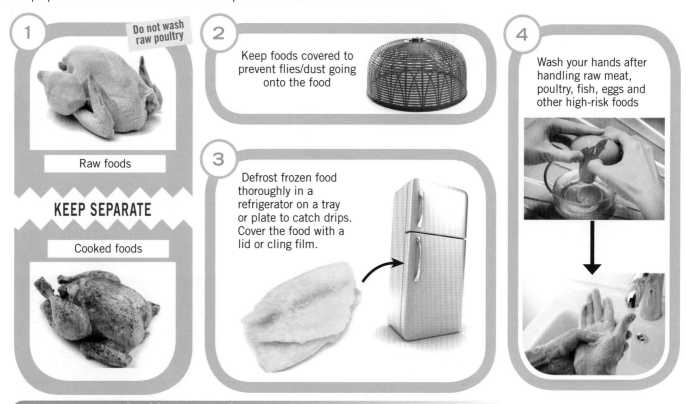

1. Do not wash raw poultry
   Raw foods
   KEEP SEPARATE
   Cooked foods

2. Keep foods covered to prevent flies/dust going onto the food

3. Defrost frozen food thoroughly in a refrigerator on a tray or plate to catch drips. Cover the food with a lid or cling film.

4. Wash your hands after handling raw meat, poultry, fish, eggs and other high-risk foods

Key terms you should try to use in your answers

Personal hygiene: following certain routines to make sure that a person does not contaminate food with bacteria from their body

Core temperature: the temperature in the centre of a piece of food

Key learning: Controlling microbial growth and multiplication

Micro-organisms need a suitable temperature, moisture, food and time to grow and multiply.

Their growth and multiplication can be controlled at different stages of food storage and preparation:

Storing food

1 Store food correctly as soon as possible after buying it

2 Do not leave high risk foods for any length of time in a warm place such as a car boot on a sunny day.

3 Check use-by and best-before dates regularly. Use up older foods first. This is called stock rotation.

4 Refrigerators and freezers:

- Check internal temperatures regularly (0° to 5°C refrigerators, –18° to –24°C freezers)
- Check door seals are working
- Defrost regularly to keep them working properly
- Place away from the cooker or boiler in a kitchen so they can work normally
- Do not leave refrigerator doors open for any length of time.

Cooking, cooling down and serving food

1 Cook food thoroughly. Core temperature = 75°C or hotter for at least 2 minutes, using a food probe

2 Hot cooked food must be kept at 63°C or above

3 Left-over hot cooked food should be cooled to 5°C or cooler within 1½–2 hours

4 Left-over cooked food must only be re-heated once to a minimum core temperature of 75°C for at least 2 minutes

5 Use **different utensils** to serve different foods to prevent cross-contamination

Using a food probe

1 Reset

2 Sterilise/use antibacterial wipe

2 Insert into core of food

4 Do not touch hot pan with probe

5 Allow temperature to stabilise **(75°C or hotter for 2 minutes)**

6 Sterilise/use antibacterial wipe after use

Revision tip

Make a set of revision cards with the key temperatures for food storage, cooking, cooling down and re-heating to help you remember them.

Applying your learning

You are going to make a main course of lamb and vegetable curry and serve it with rice and lentil dhal.

Using your knowledge about food safety, explain how you will store, prepare, cook and serve the main ingredients in the meal (meat, vegetables, rice, lentils).

You have some hot cooked rice left over from the meal, but do not want to waste it. Explain how you will deal with the rice to make sure it does not become a food safety risk.

Multiple choice challenge

Have a go at answering these questions. They are worth **one mark** each. Answers are on page 145.

1, The use-by date on food packaging applies to these foods:

- ☐ a) Soft drinks, fresh fish, fresh milk, fruit buns
- ☐ b) Soft drinks, canned fish, UHT milk, fruit buns
- ☐ c) Fresh cheesecake, fresh fish, fresh milk, cream buns
- ☐ d) Frozen cheesecake, fresh fish, fresh milk, fruit buns

2. The best-before date on food packaging applies to these foods:

- ☐ a) Potato crisps, biscuits, fresh pizzas and canned tomatoes
- ☐ b) Potato crisps, biscuits, frozen pizzas and canned tomatoes
- ☐ c) Chilled potato salad, biscuits, frozen pizzas and canned tomatoes
- ☐ d) Chilled potato salad, biscuits, fresh pizzas and canned tomatoes

3. When buying fresh fish, it should have the following qualities:

- ☐ a) A fresh smell, soft flesh, bright red gills, shiny eyes, loose scales, moist skin
- ☐ b) A fresh smell, soft flesh, bright red gills, shiny eyes, firmly attached scales, moist skin
- ☐ c) A fresh smell, firm flesh, bright red gills, shiny eyes, loose scales, slimy skin
- ☐ d) A fresh smell, firm flesh, bright red gills, firmly attached scales, moist skin

4. When buying fresh meat, it should have the following qualities:

- ☐ a) Not too much fat, fresh smell, firm springy texture, moist flesh, bright red/pink colour
- ☐ b) Not too much fat, fresh smell, firm springy texture, moist flesh, brown colour
- ☐ c) Not too much fat, fresh smell, soft texture, dry flesh, brown colour
- ☐ d) Not too much fat, fresh smell, firm springy texture, slimy flesh, bright red/pink colour

5. When buying fresh vegetables, they should have the following qualities:

- ☐ a) A soft texture, undamaged skin, no mould, bright colour
- ☐ b) A firm crisp texture, undamaged skin, no mould, bright colour
- ☐ c) A firm crisp texture, wrinkled skin, no mould, bright colour
- ☐ d) A soft texture, wrinkled skin, no mould, bright colour

6. To store food safely, the correct internal temperature of a refrigerator is:

- ☐ a) 0°C to below 5°C
- ☐ b) 0°C to below 6°C
- ☐ c) 0°C to below 8°C
- ☐ d) 0°C to below 9°C

7. In a refrigerator set at the correct temperature, bacteria are:

- ☐ a) Alive, multiplying rapidly
- ☐ b) Alive, multiplying slowly
- ☐ c) Dormant
- ☐ d) Dead

8. If stored incorrectly, strongly flavoured foods can cause other foods to become:

- ☐ a) Tinted
- ☐ b) Tainted
- ☐ c) Tempered
- ☐ d) Toasted

9. These foods do not freeze well because they become mushy and watery when they are defrosted:

- ☐ a) Cucumbers, strawberries, lettuce
- ☐ b) Courgettes, strawberries, lettuce
- ☐ c) Carrots, raspberries, lettuce

10. One of the main sources of cross-contamination of food with bacteria is:

- ☐ a) Packaging
- ☐ b) Plastics
- ☐ c) People
- ☐ d) Paper

11. To prevent cross-contamination of food with bacteria, the following practices should be followed:

- ☐ a) Keep raw and cooked foods separate in refrigerators and chilled cabinets
- ☐ b) Use separate utensils for preparing, cooking and serving raw and cooked foods
- ☐ c) Use separate work surfaces for preparing raw and cooked foods
- ☐ d) All of these

12. The core temperature of cooked food should be:

- ☐ a) 75°C for at least 1 minute
- ☐ b) 63°C for at least 2 minutes
- ☐ c) 75°C for at least 2 minutes
- ☐ d) 63°C for at least 1 minute

13. Hot cooked food must be kept at:

- ☐ a) 53°C or above
- ☐ b) 63°C or above
- ☐ c) 73°C or above
- ☐ d) 75°C or above

14. Left-over hot cooked food should be cooled to:

- ☐ a) 5°C or cooler within 2–3 hours
- ☐ b) 5°C or cooler within 1½–2 hours
- ☐ c) 8°C or cooler within 1½–2 hours
- ☐ d) 5°C or cooler within 1½–3 hours

15. Left-over cooked food must only be re-heated:

- ☐ a) Once to a minimum core temperature of 63°C for at least 2 minutes
- ☐ b) Twice to a minimum core temperature of 75°C for at least 2 minutes
- ☐ c) Once to a minimum core temperature of 70°C for at least 2 minutes
- ☐ d) Once to a minimum core temperature of 75°C for at least 2 minutes

Knowledge check – can you recall...?

(Answers on pages 149–150)

1. Three different places where food can be bought? (3 marks)
2. What use-by means? (1 mark)
3. Three examples of food that have use-by dates? (3 marks)
4. What best-before means? (1 mark)
5. Three examples of food that have best-before dates? (3 marks)
6. What 'tainted' means? (1 mark)
7. Four pieces of food safety advice to look out for on food packaging? (4 marks)
8. Four qualities to look out for when choosing to buy fresh fish? (4 marks)
9. Four qualities to look out for when choosing to buy fresh meat? (4 marks)
10. Four qualities to look out for when choosing to buy fresh fruit? (4 marks)
11. Three points to remember when storing dried foods? (3 marks)
12. Three points to remember when storing refrigerated foods? (3 marks)
13. Three points to remember when storing frozen foods? (3 marks)
14. Three types of materials that are suitable for food storage? (3 marks)
15. Ten personal hygiene rules for preparing and cooking food? (10 marks)
16. Three points to remember when handling raw and cooked foods? (3 marks)
17. One reason for covering food when preparing it? (1 mark)
18. Three occasions/activities during food preparation after which you should wash your hands? (3 marks)
19. Four food storage rules for high risk foods? (4 marks)
20. The important temperatures and times to know for:
    a) cooking food, b) keeping food hot, c) cooling down left-over hot food,
    and d) re-heating left-over food? (4 marks)

Stretch and challenge questions

1. Explain, giving detailed reasons for your answers, why food safety laws require food businesses to do the following:
   a) Send their staff for regular training about food hygiene. (4 marks)
   b) Keep rubbish bins outside and well away from a food preparation kitchen. (4 marks)
   c) Make regular checks on how well their refrigerators and freezers are working. (4 marks)

2. Giving details and examples, explain why the following are important in food storage:
   a) Food labels clearly show the shelf-life of foods. (4 marks)
   b) Cupboards for the storage of dried foods are well ventilated and pest-proof. (4 marks)
   c) Freezer and refrigerator thermometers are used. (4 marks)

3. Explain, giving detailed reasons for your answers, the food safety points you should consider for fresh red meat, e.g. beef or lamb when:
   a) Buying it. (3 marks)
   b) Storing it. (3 marks)
   c) Preparing it. (3 marks)
   d) Cooking it. (3 marks)
   e) Serving it. (3 marks)

Chapter 7: Factors affecting food choice

What do you need to know?

You now know about what foods contain, how they affect our health and well-being, how they are cooked and how to prevent them from becoming unsafe to eat.

Next you need to know:

- Which factors influence how people choose which foods they eat (**food choice**)
- How **food allergies and intolerances** can affect what people can eat
- The importance of **food labelling** and **marketing** on food choice

1 Factors that may influence what we choose to eat

Book-link:
4.1.1 Factors that influence food choice, pages 202–210

You need to know about and be able to explain which factors may influence different groups of people to choose their food. The mind map below shows the key factors that influence people about the food they choose to eat:

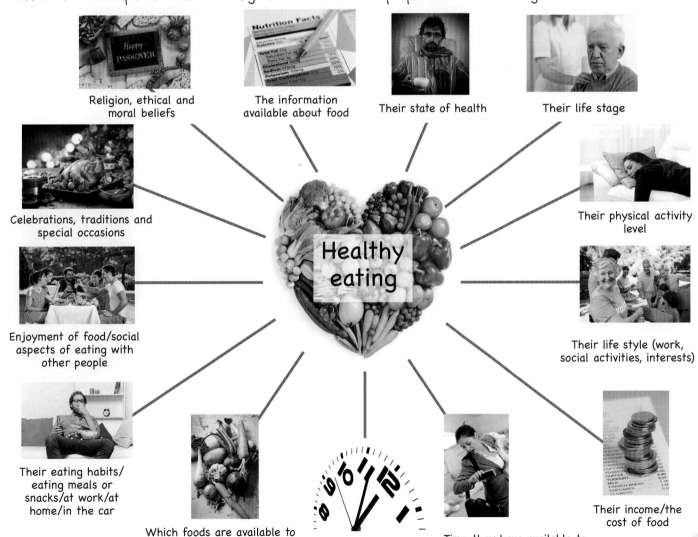

Religion, ethical and moral beliefs

The information available about food

Their state of health

Their life stage

Celebrations, traditions and special occasions

Enjoyment of food/social aspects of eating with other people

Their eating habits/ eating meals or snacks/at work/at home/in the car

Which foods are available to buy, e.g. seasonality

Time of day

Time they have available to shop, prepare and cook

Their income/the cost of food

Their life style (work, social activities, interests)

Their physical activity level

Healthy eating

ACTIVITY 7.1

For each of the case studies below, explain the factors that will influence their food choices, giving reasons for your answers:

Case study 1

Jo is a student at university and is living in a flat where the kitchen is shared with seven other people. Jo has a cupboard, one shelf in a refrigerator and one shelf in a freezer in which to store foods. Jo has a low income and limited cooking skills. Jo is allergic to nuts.

Case study 2

Mia and Karl are in their early thirties and have two young school-aged children. They both work full time and the children go to a variety of clubs after school four evenings a week. The family have a lot of bills to pay, but want the family to eat well, so try to spend their money wisely on food.

Case study 3

Dan and Amy are both 21 years old. They both work full time and like to socialise and eat out with their friends a couple of evenings in the week and at weekends. Dan is a keen gymnast and Amy plays hockey for a local team. They both like to cook when they have time.

Case study 4

An elderly couple who are both 82 years of age, live in a small flat in a town. Their only income is their state pension. They are both independent and cook their own meals. They do their own shopping and travel by public transport to purchase their groceries.

Key terms you should try to use in your answers

Lifestyle: the way in which people live, their attitudes, activities, likes and dislikes, beliefs, etc.

Seasonality: the time of the year when a particular food crop is ready to harvest and is at its best for flavour, colour and texture. It is also usually cheaper and fresher because there is a lot of it available to buy

Food miles: the distance travelled by all the ingredients in a food product until it reaches our plate

Applying your learning

Plan and make an appetising and well-balanced, one-course evening meal for a busy family with school-aged children. You have one hour in which to make and serve the meal.

Explain how you have saved time when preparing and making the meal.

Explain why it is a balanced meal.

2 Food choices

Book-link:
4.1.2 Food choices, pages 211–220

Food choices related to: Religious dietary laws

What you must know about dietary laws for different religions

In your answers, you need to know how to explain how these dietary laws influence what people can choose to eat

Buddhism	• Many are vegetarian or vegan • Avoid foods where animals were harmed • Some avoid meat and/or dairy foods • No alcohol is consumed
Christianity	• No dietary restrictions • Some Christians fast (do not eat for a period of time) • Various religious celebrations involving food, e.g. Pancake day, Lent, Good Friday, Easter, Christmas
Hinduism	• Many are vegetarian • Some practise fasting • Cow is sacred so beef is not eaten • Onions and garlic only eaten occasionally • No alcohol is consumed by many Hindus • Various religious celebrations involving food, e.g. Holi, Diwali
Islam	• Dietary laws written in Qur'an • Lawful food is 'halal' • Pork, pork products and alcohol are not consumed • Various religious celebrations involving food, e.g. Ramadan, Eid-ul-Fitr
Judaism	• Jewish food laws called Kashrut • Food that is allowed is 'Kosher' • Pork, shellfish not eaten • Dairy foods and meat must not be prepared or cooked together • Various religious celebrations involving food, e.g. Yom Kippur, Passover, Rosh Hashanah
Rastafarianism	• Dietary laws are called I-tal • Food must be natural and clean and include plenty of fruit and vegetables • Pork, fish longer than 30cm are not eaten; many do not drink alcohol, milk or coffee • Religious celebrations involving food: Ethiopian Christmas (7 January)
Sikhism	• Many Sikhs are vegetarian • Some Sikhs do not drink alcohol, tea or coffee • Religious celebrations involving food, e.g. Gurpurbs

ACTIVITY 7.2

Using your knowledge of the dietary laws of different religions, match up each religion with the correct foods that are allowed or not allowed to be eaten:

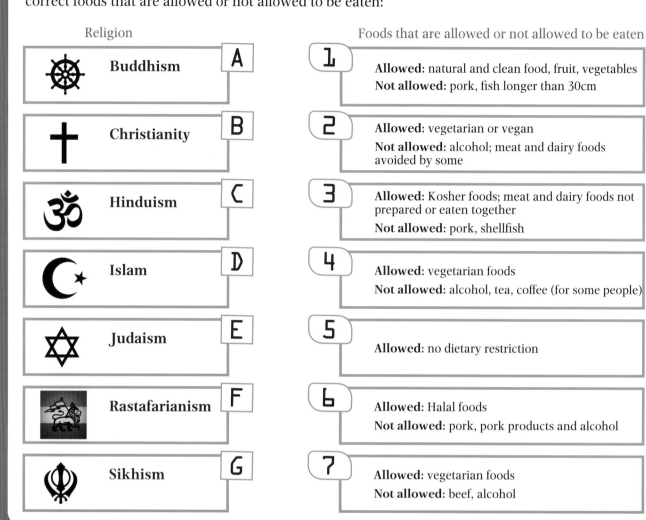

Religion		Foods that are allowed or not allowed to be eaten
Buddhism	A	**1** — **Allowed:** natural and clean food, fruit, vegetables; **Not allowed:** pork, fish longer than 30cm
Christianity	B	**2** — **Allowed:** vegetarian or vegan; **Not allowed:** alcohol; meat and dairy foods avoided by some
Hinduism	C	**3** — **Allowed:** Kosher foods; meat and dairy foods not prepared or eaten together; **Not allowed:** pork, shellfish
Islam	D	**4** — **Allowed:** vegetarian foods; **Not allowed:** alcohol, tea, coffee (for some people)
Judaism	E	**5** — **Allowed:** no dietary restriction
Rastafarianism	F	**6** — **Allowed:** Halal foods; **Not allowed:** pork, pork products and alcohol
Sikhism	G	**7** — **Allowed:** vegetarian foods; **Not allowed:** beef, alcohol

Food choices related to: Ethical and moral beliefs about food

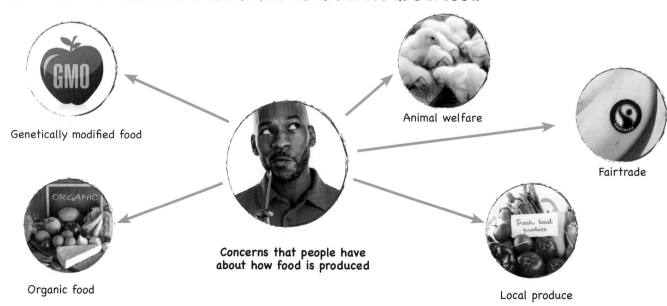

Genetically modified food

Animal welfare

Fairtrade

Organic food

Concerns that people have about how food is produced

Local produce

98

What you must know about food choices linked to ethical and moral beliefs

In your answers, you need to know how to explain what people believe is right or wrong about these issues

Animal welfare	• How well animals are reared and looked after
Fairtrade production	• Making sure farmers in developing countries are paid fairly for their crops and their workers live in good conditions
Intensive farming	• Use of pesticides/effects on the environment/conditions in which animals, birds and fish are kept/using up lots of land to grow crops and animal feed/using up natural resources such as water
Genetically modified food	• Effects on the environment/whether or not humans should alter food in this way/it may affect people who have food allergies
Local produce	• Few **food miles**/supports local producers/seasonal food/may be cheaper
Organic food production	• Grown without use of fertilisers/virtually no pesticides used/better for the environment and soil

Food choices related to food intolerances and allergies

Both are medical conditions which limit what people can choose to eat.

Food intolerance

Food intolerance is hard to diagnose.

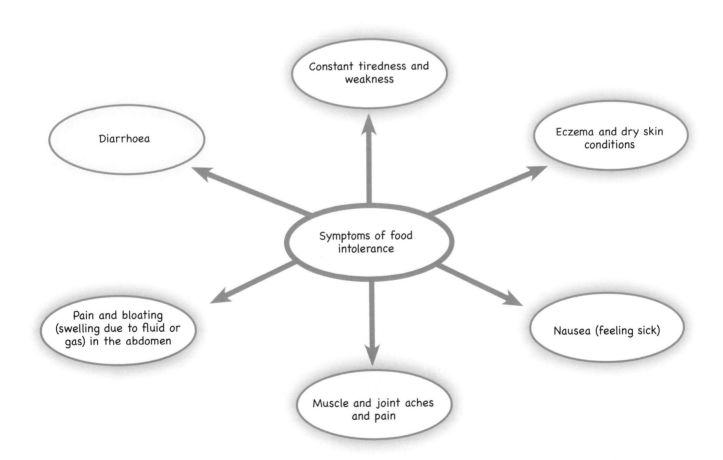

What you must know about food intolerance

In your answers, you need to know how to explain what food intolerance is and how it affects food choices

Lactose intolerance

- Lactose = natural sugar in milk
- People with lactose intolerance cannot digest it, so bacteria in the large intestine break it down
- This causes bloating, flatulence, abdominal pain, diarrhoea, nausea
- Lactose intolerant people must avoid drinking milk, and eating milk products
- It is possible to buy lactose-free dairy products, e.g. milk and yogurt

Coeliac disease (gluten intolerance)

- Coeliacs have an intolerance to the protein **gluten**
- Gluten is found in wheat, oats, barley and rye – coeliacs must avoid any food that contains them
- In the small intestine, **villi** line the inside and nutrients are absorbed through them into the bloodstream
- Gluten intolerance causes the villi to become very small and deformed so not enough nutrients are absorbed

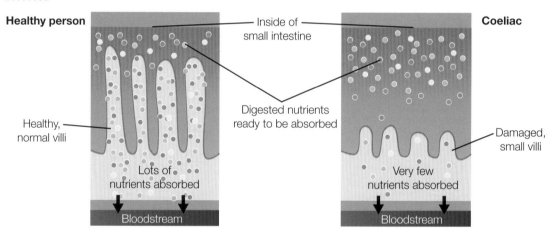

This causes the coeliac to become malnourished – they have these symptoms:

- anaemia
- lack of energy
- tiredness
- weight loss
- children do not grow properly

- Coeliacs must avoid any food containing gluten
- Many gluten free food products are available in food shops
- Coeliacs can eat agar, almonds, buckwheat, carrageenan, cassava (manioc/tapioca), chestnuts, corn (maize), linseeds, gram flour, millet, polenta, potato flour, peas, beans, lentils, quinoa, rice, sago, sorghum, soya flour, lentil flour

Applying your learning

Plan and make a two-course dinner for a friend who is a coeliac.

Explain how you have adapted the recipe(s) to avoid including gluten in the meal.

Food allergy

What you must know about food allergy

In your answers, you need to know how to explain what food allergy is and how it affects food choices

Food allergy
- Someone with a food allergy has a serious reaction to certain foods or ingredients in foods
- This can happen in a few seconds, minutes or hours after eating the food
- It can be life-threatening
- An allergic reaction is caused by the **immune system** in body reacting and producing **histamine** which causes various symptoms: skin rashes, itchy skin, nose and eyes, wheezing, coughing, swollen lips, eyelids, face
- **Anaphylactic shock** – severe and dangerous reaction – mouth and throat swell, cannot breathe, swallow or speak properly – must have medical treatment immediately

Swollen lips caused by a food allergy

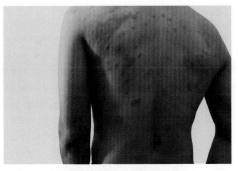
Skin rash caused by a food allergy

Food allergens
- An allergen is something that causes the symptoms of a food allergy
- Common foods that cause allergic reactions include: eggs, milk, fish, shellfish, peanuts, other nuts, seeds, soya, some preservatives, strawberries, kiwi fruit, celery, celeriac, mustard, preservatives (sulphur dioxide and sulphites)
- Someone who is allergic to one or more foods must avoid eating them and read food labels very carefully in case they appear in the ingredients list
- Known food allergens must be shown on a food label by law

Common food allergens

Key terms you should try to use in your answers

Food intolerance: a long-term condition where after several hours or days, certain foods cause a person to feel unwell and have a range of symptoms, but it is usually not life threatening and does not involve the immune system

Food allergy: this happens to some people when their immune system has a very sensitive reaction to specific foods, which causes severe and potentially life-threatening symptoms that happen very quickly after the food is eaten

Food labelling and marketing influences

What you must know about food labelling

In your answers, you need to know how to explain why food labels are used and what they have to show

Food labelling
- They give consumers information so they can make informed food choices
- They are used to attract consumers to buy a product
- They are designed to be eye-catching, colourful, have attention-grabbing names, words and slogans to appeal to different target groups
- Food labels must be clear, easy to read and understand and must not mislead the consumer about the food inside
- They **protect** the consumer and food manufacturer by giving certain information by law:
  - The name and description of the food product
  - Ingredients list (in descending order by quantity in the food)
  - Net quantity (weight or volume) of the food (i.e. the amount of food you actually have to eat)
  - Name and address of food manufacturer, distributor or retailer
  - The place of origin of the food
  - How to store, prepare and cook the product (food safety)
  - The shelf-life (use-by and best before dates)
  - Allergy warnings
  - Information about additives put into the food

Nutrition information on food labels
- Food manufacturers have been required by law to show this since December 2016
- Labels **must** show the following information for every 100g/100ml *and* serving quantity of a food or drink product:
  - Energy value (kJ or kcal)
  - Protein (g)
  - Total fat (g)
  - Saturated fat (g)
  - Total carbohydrate (g)
  - Sugars (g)
  - Salt (g)
- Manufacturers can also show other nutrients, e.g. starch, fibre, vitamins, minerals
- Traffic light system – developed to show consumers at a glance whether a product has a low, medium or high amount of fat, saturated fat, sugars or salt by using traffic light colours: **green for LOW**, amber for MEDIUM, **red for HIGH**
- Nutritional labelling helps consumers to understand what a food contains and how it contributes to healthy eating

ACTIVITY 7.3

Using your knowledge of food labelling, identify which information on the food label below is required by law. Explain how each piece of information will help to the consumer to choose their food.

Only responsibly sourced fish used in this product

Sea shanty pie

By one, get second half price

Serves 2

600g

Use by 22nd March 2017

Haddock, salmon and prawns in a parsley sauce, topped with creamy mashed potato and cheese

Nutritional information:

	Per 100g	Per 300g serving
Energy value (kJ or kcal)	85 kcal/356kJ	255kcal/1,068kJ
Protein (g)	9.5g	28.5g
Total fat (g)	1.9g	5.7g
Saturated fat (g)	0.7g	2.1g
Total carbohydrate (g)	11g	33g
Sugars (g)	1.8g	5.4g
Salt (g)	0.2g	0.6g
Fibre (g)	1.2g	3.6g

Storage
Keep refrigerated.
Consume by the use-by date.
Suitable for freezing.

Preparation and cooking:
Remove outer cardboard sleeve and plastic film. Place product on a baking tray and bake at 200°C/ gas 6 for 30 minutes, until golden brown on top and piping hot.

Ingredients: Potatoes, milk, haddock, salmon, prawns, cheese, flour, butter, parsley, ground black pepper, salt

No artificial colourings, flavourings or preservative.

Allergy information
Contains shellfish, milk, gluten, cheese and wheat flour

SLEEVE
CARD
widely recycled

TRAY
PLASTIC
check local recycling

FILM
PLASTIC
not currently recycled

Made in the UK using salmon and prawns farmed in Scotland and haddock responsibly sourced from the North Atlantic

L. Goodfoods Ltd., Unit 8, London Way, Anytown, UK.

What you must know about food marketing methods

In your answers, you need to know how to explain why and how marketing is used and how it influences consumers' food choice

Marketing in different media

- **Marketing** = advertising and promoting food products to encourage groups of consumers to buy particular products

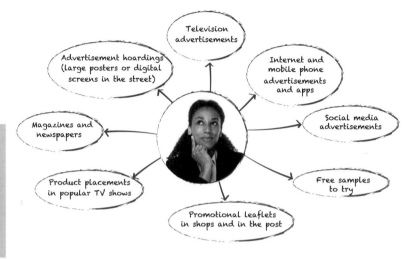

Price deals and special offers

- **Special offers:** buy one get one free (BOGOF), buy 2 get 3rd free, buy 1 get 2nd half price, special promotion/buy, price reduction, meal deals, limited editions
- Often the food producer has to pay for the cost of supermarket special offers
- Special offers may encourage consumers to buy more food than they need, so some may be wasted
- It is important to compare the price per 100g/100ml of the special offer with a similar food that is not on offer (e.g. cheddar cheese), to make sure that you really are saving money
- Special offers are often targeted to children and young people
- **'Pester power'** means encouraging children to pester their parents into buying a product
- Bright colours, e.g. red and yellow are often used on food labels and signs to attract people to buy special offers

Different price bands

- Different prices for similar products are often available, e.g. sausages. The cheapest is the 'value brand' and the most expensive is the top of the range (e.g. 'best', 'finest')
- Simple packaging is used for value products
- Colours associated with expensive items are often used for top of the range products, e.g. silver, gold, purple, dark green, black

Loyalty cards

- These are used to target consumer buying habits and advertise products to them
- Consumers with loyalty cards are often sent money off vouchers of food they have recently purchased encouraging them to shop at a particular store

Linking a product

- Products are often linked to a celebrity, e.g. a pop star, cartoon character or sports personality or a famous brand, e.g. a film company

Ethical marketing

- Products are often marketed as being Fairtrade, organic, local produce; or having recyclable packaging, low carbon footprint

Healthy eating

- Foods are marketed for special diets, added nutrients, reduced amounts of, e.g. fat, salt or sugar

Time saving

- Foods are marketed as being convenient and saving effort

ACTIVITY 7.4

Using your knowledge of how foods are marketed to consumers, look at the foods below and list the method(s) you think are being used to market the foods and the target market(s) for each. Here is an example to help you:

A new brand of low-fat, fruit flavoured yogurt

The marketing methods that could be used to promote the yogurt may include:

Price deal: e.g. a lower introductory price/buy one, get one free/buy two get third free/buy one get second half price

Healthy eating: to promote the yogurt as containing less fat than other brands

Ethical marketing: the yogurt may be made with local ingredients/the packaging may be recyclable

Marketed in different media: e.g. phone apps, TV, advertising leaflet, free sample, and coupon with money off

1  Reduced sugar and salt baked beans

6  Value brand sausages and top end of the range sausages

2  Fair trade cocoa or coffee

7 Recycling label on a food label

3  Organic vegetables

8 Product with a special offer logo

4 Vegetables grown locally

5 Food products with a celebrity chef endorsement/ cartoon character

9   Convenience foods, e.g. ready-made soup, salad in a bag or box, ready prepared fruit

Key terms you should try to use in your answers

Target group: a specific group of similar people, e.g. all the same age, with similar jobs, such as students

Marketing: advertising and promoting a food product to encourage people to buy it

Revision tip

To help you remember and apply what you know about food labelling and marketing, look at the labels on a variety of food products at home or in a shop and identify:

- What information on them is required by law.
- Who the target group(s) are for the products.
- Which marketing methods have been used to promote the products.

Multiple choice challenge

Have a go at answering these questions. They are worth **one mark** each. Answers are on page 145.

1. The dietary laws in Hinduism do not allow the following meat to be eaten:
   - a) Pork
   - b) Beef
   - c) Chicken
   - d) Lamb

2. The dietary laws in Islam do not allow the following meat to be eaten:
   - a) Pork
   - b) Beef
   - c) Chicken
   - d) Lamb

3. The dietary laws in Judaism do not allow the following meat to be eaten:
   - a) Chicken
   - b) Beef
   - c) Pork
   - d) Lamb

4. The dietary laws in Rastafarianism do not allow the following meat to be eaten:
   - a) Pork
   - b) Beef
   - c) Chicken
   - d) Lamb

5. People with lactose intolerance should avoid eating:
   - a) Eggs
   - b) Shellfish
   - c) Milk products
   - d) Bread

6. A person who has gluten intolerance is called a:
   - a) Candidate
   - b) Coeliac
   - c) Vegan
   - d) Diabetic

7. In gluten intolerance, nutrients cannot be properly absorbed in the:
   - a) Large intestine
   - b) Liver
   - c) Small intestine
   - d) Bowel

8. A severe allergic reaction to nuts can cause:
   - a) Lactose intolerance
   - b) Diarrhoea
   - c) Anaphylactic shock
   - d) Beri beri

9. These foods are common food allergens:
   - a) Peanuts, eggs, shellfish, sesame seeds
   - b) Peanuts, beef, shellfish, sesame seeds
   - c) Peanuts, eggs, pork, sesame seeds
   - d) Peanuts, lettuce, shellfish, sesame seeds

10. By law in the UK, food labels must show:
   - a) Ingredients list, shelf-life, storage instructions, the price
   - b) Marketing slogan, shelf-life, storage instructions, the price
   - c) Ingredients list, shelf-life, storage instructions, net quantity
   - d) Ingredients list, shelf-life, opening instructions, storage instructions

Knowledge check – can you recall...?

(Answers on pages 150–151)

1. Eight different factors that influence what people choose to eat? *(8 marks)*
2. What seasonality means? *(1 mark)*
3. What food miles means? *(1 mark)*
4. What best-before means? *(1 mark)*
5. What snacking and grazing mean? *(1 mark)*
6. Four different social occasions where food plays an important part? *(4 marks)*
7. The dietary rules for four different religions? *(4 marks)*
8. Six general symptoms of food intolerance? *(6 marks)*
9. Three foods to avoid if a person has lactose intolerance? *(3 marks)*
10. Four symptoms of coeliac disease? *(4 marks)*
11. Four foods that coeliacs can eat? *(4 marks)*
12. Five foods that can cause food allergy? *(5 marks)*
13. Two symptoms of anaphylactic shock? *(2 marks)*
14. Six pieces of information required by law on a food label? *(6 marks)*
15. What nutritional information must be shown on a food label? *(7 marks)*
16. Five ways in which foods are marketed through different media? *(5 marks)*
17. Five methods that are used to market foods? *(5 marks)*
18. What pester power means? *(1 mark)*
19. Two reasons why food labels are used? *(2 marks)*
20. What marketing means? *(1 mark)*

Stretch and challenge questions

1. There are several factors that influence what people choose to eat.

   For each of the examples below, choose three factors and explain, giving reasons, how these would influence what each person would choose to eat:

   a) A middle-aged man who has high blood pressure. *(3 marks)*

   b) A young man who follows a vegan diet and works for a charity that supports farmers in developing countries. *(3 marks)*

   c) A busy young woman who likes to eat well, but has little time to cook her own meals. *(3 marks)*

2. Food labels are used for the majority of the foods that we buy.

   a) Give two reasons why food labels are used. *(2 marks)*

   b) Give five pieces of information that have to be on a food label by law and explain how each helps the consumer to choose their food. *(10 marks)*

3. Food products are marketed to consumers to encourage them to buy them.

   a) List three ways in which a supermarket may market food products to its customers. *(3 marks)*

   b) List three ways in which a food manufacturer may market a new food product to consumers. *(3 marks)*

Chapter 8: British and International Cuisines

What do you need to know?

You now know about the various things that influence the food choices people make.

Next you need to know:

- The influence of **traditional cuisines** around the world on food choice
- The types of foods and ingredients used in traditional cuisines around the world
- The ways in which foods are prepared, cooked and served in different cuisines

1 Traditional cuisines

Book-link:
4.2.1 Traditional cuisines, pages 237–246

You need to know about and be able to give examples of different features, characteristics and dishes from British and International cuisines.

The revision map below explains what a cuisine is:

People bring traditional eating habits which become part of the cuisine of the country they migrate to

Local geography and climate

Affects what food is grown and is available to catch/gather

Influenced by

Immigration of people from other countries

CUISINE = a particular style of cooking and eating found in a country or region of the world developed over many centuries

Distinctive ingredients

Cuisines traditionally use

Distinctive presentation and/or serving techniques

Specific preparation and cooking methods

Specific equipment for cooking and serving food

ACTIVITY 8.1

Produce a revision map for a country of your choice, e.g. India, Italy.

Include on the revision map:

- Distinctive ingredients
- Specific equipment for cooking and serving food
- Specific preparation, presentation and cooking methods
- Examples of traditional dishes.

ACTIVITY 8.2

Cuisine picture search.

Look at the images in the picture search below. For each of the countries in the following chart, identify and write down the numbers of three images that are typical of their cuisine.

Country	Which images?	Can you name the foods/dishes?
England		
Italy		
Japan		
Mexico		
Denmark		
Spain		

Applying your learning

Plan and make two traditional recipes.

List the ingredients, preparation and cooking methods, equipment and ways of serving the recipes that are specific to that cuisine.

Food spoilage and contamination

Multiple choice challenge

Have a go at answering these questions. They are worth **one mark** each. Answers are on page 145.

1. In which cuisine is a tagine used?

- [ ] a) Spanish
- [ ] b) Mexican
- [ ] c) Norwegian
- [ ] d) Moroccan

2. In which cuisine is a sushi mat used?

- [ ] a) French
- [ ] b) Japanese
- [ ] c) Russian
- [ ] d) Welsh

3. In which cuisine is a wok mainly used?

- [ ] a) Spanish
- [ ] b) Mexican
- [ ] c) Chinese
- [ ] d) Moroccan

4. Tiramisu, panna cotta and panettone are sweet dishes from which cuisine?

- [ ] a) Greek
- [ ] b) Mexican
- [ ] c) Chinese
- [ ] d) Italian

5. Which of the following cheeses are eaten in French cuisine?

- [ ] a) Cheshire, cheddar, stilton
- [ ] b) Edam, gouda, beemster
- [ ] c) Roquefort, camembert, brie
- [ ] d) Formaggella, gorgonzola, parmesan

6. Which of the following ingredients are commonly used in Thai cuisine?

- [ ] a) Pasta, tomatoes, olives, rice
- [ ] b) Sticky rice, coconut milk, lemongrass, chilli peppers
- [ ] c) Wheat flour, butter, cheese, potatoes
- [ ] d) Seafood, chorizo, serrano ham, paprika

7. Which of the following is the name of an Italian pasta shape?

- [ ] a) Tortellini
- [ ] b) Conchiglie
- [ ] c) Tagliatelle
- [ ] d) All of these

8. Which of the following ingredients are commonly used in Moroccan cuisine?

- [ ] a) Pasta, tomatoes, olives, rice
- [ ] b) Sticky rice, coconut milk, lemongrass, chilli peppers
- [ ] c) Couscous, lamb, aubergines, fava beans
- [ ] d) Seafood, chorizo, serrano ham, paprika

9. Biryani, dahl, kofta and jalfrezi are all the names of regional dishes in which country?

- [ ] a) Kenya
- [ ] b) China
- [ ] c) Portugal
- [ ] d) India

10. Popcorn, brownies, peanut butter and cornbread are all foods that were developed in the cuisine of which country?

- [ ] a) Canada
- [ ] b) Brazil
- [ ] c) USA
- [ ] d) Mexico

Knowledge check – can you recall...?

(Answers on page 151)

1. The definition of the word 'cuisine'?   *(1 mark)*
2. Two main influences on the development of cuisines?   *(2 marks)*
3. Three distinctive features of meal preparation that have resulted in cuisines being developed in a particular way (e.g. using specific cooking methods)?   *(3 marks)*

Stretch and challenge questions

1. The cuisines of many countries have been influenced by people from other countries coming to live there and bringing their traditional foods and eating habits with them.

    Giving details and examples, explain how and why the UK has been influenced by the cuisines of other countries in the last few decades.   *(12 marks)*

2. Research has shown that the Mediterranean cuisine is considered to be very healthy.

    a) Describe what types of ingredients and meals are eaten in Mediterranean cuisine, including the preparation and cooking methods that are used.   *(5 marks)*

    b) Using your knowledge of nutrition, explain why the Mediterranean diet is so good for health.   *(5 marks)*

Chapter 9: Sensory evaluation

What do you need to know?

You now know about the influence of traditional cuisines on food choice.

Next you need to know:

- How the **senses** of **sight, smell, taste, touch and hearing** influence our food choice
- How **sensory evaluation** methods are used to measure the sensory qualities of food

---

1 **How the senses influence food choice**

Book-link:
4.3.1 Sensory evaluation, pages 247–254

- There are five senses – sight, smell, taste, touch and sound
- All the senses work together so we can enjoy food
- Food needs to be presented so it is appetising (make people want to eat it)
- Well-presented food should:
  - look and smell good
  - have a good flavour and texture
  - sound right (e.g. crusty/crisp).

The revision maps below explains how the senses influence the choice and enjoyment of food:

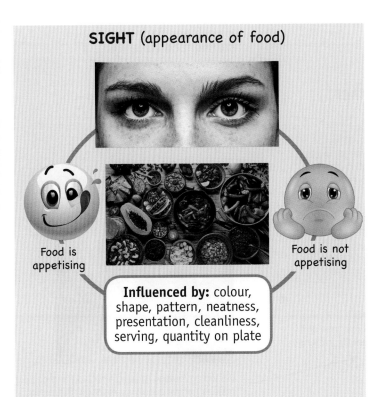

SIGHT (appearance of food)

Food is appetising

Food is not appetising

Influenced by: colour, shape, pattern, neatness, presentation, cleanliness, serving, quantity on plate

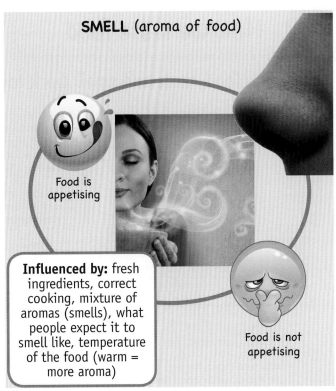

SMELL (aroma of food)

Food is appetising

Food is not appetising

Influenced by: fresh ingredients, correct cooking, mixture of aromas (smells), what people expect it to smell like, temperature of the food (warm = more aroma)

TASTE (flavour of food)

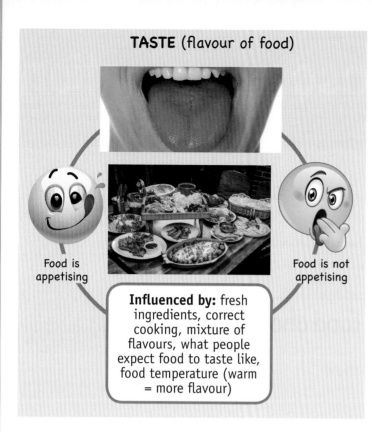

Food is appetising

Food is not appetising

Influenced by: fresh ingredients, correct cooking, mixture of flavours, what people expect food to taste like, food temperature (warm = more flavour)

TOUCH (texture and mouthfeel of food)

Food is appetising

Food is not appetising

Influenced by: fresh ingredients, correct preparation and cooking, no unexpected textures, e.g. lumps/bones/shells/stalks

SOUND (e.g. crispy, crunchy, fizzy)

Food is appetising

Food is not appetising

Influenced by: colour, shape, fresh ingredients – stale foods lose crispness crunch and fizziness, storing food correctly

2 How we taste food

To enjoy food, taste and smell work together:

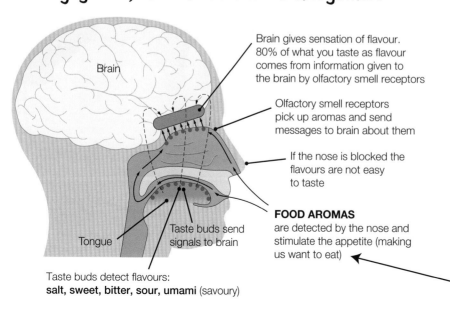

Brain

Brain gives sensation of flavour. 80% of what you taste as flavour comes from information given to the brain by olfactory smell receptors

Olfactory smell receptors pick up aromas and send messages to brain about them

If the nose is blocked the flavours are not easy to taste

FOOD AROMAS are detected by the nose and stimulate the appetite (making us want to eat)

Tongue

Taste buds send signals to brain

Taste buds detect flavours: **salt, sweet, bitter, sour, umami** (savoury)

Chopping/cutting/grating/crushing and cooking release natural chemicals in foods as aromas

Key terms you should try to use in your answers

Appetising: food prepared, cooked and served so well that you want to eat it

Olfactory (smell) receptors: special cells in the nose that pick up aromas (smells)

Senses: the ability of the body to react to things through sight, taste, hearing, smell (aroma) and touch

Sensory analysis: a way of measuring the sensory qualities of food

Sensory descriptors: words used to describe the characteristics of a food

Taste buds: special cells on the tongue that pick up flavours

THEORY INTO PRACTICE
– try this practical challenge

Plan and make a two-course evening meal for two adults, which demonstrates the sensory characteristics (flavours, aromas, textures, appearance and sounds) of a cuisine of your choice, e.g. Indian, Moroccan, Chinese, Spanish.

QUESTIONS

Using your knowledge of preparation and cooking methods:

- Explain how the flavours and aromas of the ingredients you have used have been released and combined to make the food appetising and enjoyable.   *(3 marks)*

- Explain how you are going to present the meal in order to make it look interesting and appetising.   *(3 marks)*

- Explain how the preparation and cooking methods used will preserve/develop the textures of the ingredients to make the meal interesting and appetising.   *(3 marks)*

ACTIVITY 9.1

Sensory descriptors are used to describe the characteristics of a food.

For each of the following foods, describe the characteristics you would expect using sensory descriptors. An example is given below (the sensory descriptors are highlighted):

A freshly baked loaf of bread: Freshly baked bread should have a crusty, chewy outer layer, which is golden brown in colour. The inside of the loaf should be soft and light in texture, and be a little moist. The loaf should have a fresh, slightly yeasty smell and the crust should have a characteristic toasted smell due to the action of dry heat on the starch which turns to dextrin in the oven. When the loaf is tapped with the finger, it should sound hollow which means it is cooked right through.

Have a go at describing these foods. Imagine you are describing them to someone who has never seen or tasted these foods before. You must be as descriptive as possible – remember not to use words such as 'lovely', 'horrible', 'nice', as these are your opinion, not descriptive words.

1. A grilled beef burger
2. Sautéed onions
3. A cheese scone
4. A shortbread biscuit
5. A baked jacket potato
6. A lemon meringue pie
7. A lamb curry with rice
8. A fresh orange
9. A choux pastry éclair
10. A chocolate mousse

Sensory testing methods

Sensory testing methods are used by food manufacturers, chefs and food retailers:

- To test the acceptability and popularity of new products

- To evaluate food products that might have been changed in some way, e.g. a new flavour, a different texture

- Different types of sensory tests are used:

- **Preference tests:** to find out which food product people **prefer** (like best)

- **Discriminatory tests:** to find out whether people can **tell the difference** between similar food samples

- **Grading tests:** to find out the **order** in which people like a set of food samples or a specific characteristic of a food product e.g. sweetness, saltiness

Randomly coded biscuit samples ready to be tried in a food tasting panel

How to ensure a fair test when setting up a food tasting panel:

Advice for setting up and carrying out a sensory analysis tasting panel	Reasons
Use a quiet area away from food preparation and cooking activities	To avoid food tasters being disturbed and influenced by other people
Use 5–10 people as testers – they should work on their own	To ensure realistic results and make sure they are not influenced by other people's opinions
Use hygienic conditions, e.g. separate spoons/samples for each taster	To avoid contamination by micro-organisms
Give clear instructions to the testers	So that they know exactly what they need to do
Give charts to food tasters so they can fill them in as they taste the food	So that you can keep an accurate record of the results of the panel
Give tasters water or plain crackers to drink or eat between different food samples	To clear their taste buds so they do not get confused between samples
Food samples should be coded randomly with numbers or letters. Only the person setting up the tasting panel should know which code applies to which food sample	So that food tasters do not know which sample is which, to ensure a fair test (called a blind test)
Give tasters small samples, and same sized servings of food	To prevent food tasters filling up and not tasting all the samples properly
Samples should be presented/served at the same temperature	To prevent the flavours being affected and so that tasters can taste them comfortably
Samples should be presented/served on the same coloured plates usually black or white	To prevent the taster's senses from being distracted or influenced by background colour and appearance of the food samples

Multiple choice challenge

Have a go at answering these questions. They are worth **one mark** each. Answers are on page 145.

1. **The five senses that influence food choice are:**
   - a) Sight, smell, taste, digestion and sound
   - b) Sight, smell, taste, touch and sound
   - c) Sight, smell, taste, touch and breathing
   - d) Sight, smell, temperature, touch and sound

2. **The following visual characteristics (appearance) influence the enjoyment of food:**
   - a) Colour, price, shape, quantity, neatness, aroma, cleanliness
   - b) Colour, pattern, shape, quantity, flavour, presentation, cleanliness
   - c) Colour, pattern, shape, quantity, neatness, sound, cleanliness
   - d) Colour, pattern, shape, quantity, neatness, presentation, cleanliness

3. **Which of the following might spoil the enjoyment and sensory qualities of a béchamel sauce?**
   - a) Glossy appearance
   - b) Smooth texture
   - c) Lumps of flour
   - d) Pouring consistency

4. **What will happen to the sensory characteristics of some shortbread biscuits that are stored for a few weeks in an opened packet inside a kitchen cupboard?**
   - a) Their flavour will intensify and they will become hard
   - b) Their texture will soften and they will taste stale
   - c) They will become darker in colour and soft in texture
   - d) Their texture will harden and they will taste stale

5. **What are olfactory receptors?**
   - a) Special cells in the eyes to help us see
   - b) Special cells on the tongue to help us taste
   - c) Special cells in the nose to help us smell
   - d) Special cells in the ears that help us hear

6. **What type of flavour is umami?**
   - a) Sweet
   - b) Savoury
   - c) Sour
   - d) Bitter

7. **To enjoy the flavour of foods, these two senses work together:**
   - a) Sight and sound
   - b) Sight and smell
   - c) Taste and sight
   - d) Smell and taste

8. **What will happen to the sensory characteristics of a piece of meat that is grilled for too long?**
   - a) It will become tender and moist
   - b) It will become tough and dry
   - c) It will become tough and moist
   - d) It will become tender and dry

9. **What will happen to the sensory characteristics of a piece of frozen cucumber when it is defrosted?**
   - a) It will become mushy and dry and lose its shape
   - b) It will become crisp and moist and keep its shape
   - c) It will become mushy and watery and lose its shape
   - d) It will become crisp and dry and keep its shape

10. **The following words are all good sensory descriptors of foods:**
    - a) Crisp, sweet, tender, moist
    - b) Nice, horrible, tender, nasty
    - c) Crisp, nice, tender, moist
    - d) Crisp, sweet, tender, nasty

Knowledge check – can you recall...?

(Answers on pages 151–152)

1. What the five senses are? *(5 marks)*
2. What 'appetising' means? *(1 mark)*
3. What sensory descriptors are? *(1 mark)*
4. How the senses of taste and smell work together? *(5 marks)*
5. What olfactory receptors are? *(1 mark)*
6. What taste buds are? *(1 mark)*
7. Two ways in which aromas are released from foods? *(2 marks)*
8. What sensory analysis is? *(1 mark)*
9. Three different types of sensory analysis tests? *(3 marks)*
10. Five ways of ensuring a realistic and controlled test when setting up a food tasting panel? *(5 marks)*

Stretch and challenge questions

1. Using your knowledge of the functional and chemical properties of foods and different cooking methods, explain in detail, how the sensory qualities of foods can be preserved, improved or spoiled when preparing and cooking the following foods:

   a) Green vegetables, e.g. broccoli, Brussels sprouts, green cabbage.   *(4 marks)*

   b) Meat.   *(4 marks)*

   c) White rice.   *(4 marks)*

2. Using your knowledge of the chemical properties of foods and different food storage methods, explain in detail, how the following foods should be stored in order to preserve their sensory qualities:

   a) Savoury crackers and crispbreads.   *(4 marks)*

   b) Salad vegetables, e.g. lettuce, cucumber, peppers.   *(4 marks)*

   c) Eggs.   *(4 marks)*

3. A local farm shop is developing a new ice cream to be launched in winter. The chefs will be carrying out some sensory testing on the new flavour, which is cinnamon and cranberry. Explain, giving reasons:

   a) Which sensory test they will use.   *(1 mark)*

   b) Eight sensory descriptors that could be included on a tasting chart for the new ice cream.   *(8 marks)*

   c) How the sensory analysis test will be carried out.   *(5 marks)*

   d) The controlled conditions which will be required to ensure fair testing.   *(5 marks)*

Chapter 10: Environmental impact and sustainability

What do you need to know?

You now know about the many ways in which our individual food choices are influenced and how our choices affect our health and well-being.

Next you need to know:

- What **food provenance** means: where and how foods are **grown, reared, gathered** and **caught**
- The effects of our **food choices** and **food production** on the **global environment**
- How **climate change** affects food production and availability
- How the supply of food for the world's population can be made more **sustainable**

1 Food provenance

Book-link:
5.1.1 Food sources, pages 255–262

- Food provenance means where foods and ingredients come from
- Food production can have impacts on the environment
- Having information about how and where food is grown/reared/gathered/caught helps people to choose their food

Here is a revision mind map to help you learn about food provenance:

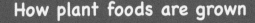
How plant foods are grown

Intensive farming		Organic farming

Intensive farming

Plant crops grown in large fields / glass houses / poly-tunnels
Same crop grown on a piece of land

Artificial fertilisers used to help crops grow

Pesticides used to prevent attack by moulds, insects, etc.

Large machinery used to manage crops

Organic farming

Crop rotation – i.e. different crops grown on same piece of land each year

Crops fertilised with manure and compost

Pesticide use is severely restricted

Natural predators encouraged, e.g. ladybirds to eat aphids

Needs lots of manual labour (people) to remove weeds and manage the crops

Soil Association sets standards for organic production

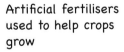
soil Association

How animal foods are reared

Intensive farming

Livestock (animals, birds, fish) reared in large numbers often indoors in large sheds/cages/tanks (keeps costs down)

Often fed on man-made foods

May pick up diseases from other animals so may be given drugs, antibiotics, growth promoters and other medicines

May become stressed because not used to living in large numbers

Organic farming

Livestock kept in small numbers often outside (free range)

Must be fed on organically produced foods

Must not be given drugs, antibiotics, growth promoters; can be given medicines by a vet if ill

Animals live as naturally as possible

Animal welfare standards are set to ensure that they are well looked after

Hunting and gathering foods from the wild

Plants

Seaweed (e.g. kelp), herbs, fruits (e.g. blackberries), mushrooms, honey

Animals

Animals: e.g. deer (venison), boar (pig), snails, rabbits, hare
Birds: e.g. pheasants, grouse, quail
Fish: e.g. salmon, trout and seafood e.g. mussels, oysters

Key terms you should try to use in your answers

Food provenance: where foods and ingredients originally come from

Pesticides: chemicals sprayed onto plant crops to:
- prevent insect and mould attack
- prevent weed growth
- produce strong plants

Grown ingredients: plants grown for food (herbs, fruits, vegetables, cereals)

Reared ingredients: animals, birds and fish specially bred in captivity and brought up to be ready to eat

Gathered ingredients: plant foods gathered from the wild for eating (e.g. herbs, edible fungi, berries, seaweed)

Caught ingredients: animals, birds, fish and shellfish hunted and caught from the wild for eating

Intensive farming: growing or rearing large numbers of the same type of plants or animals in one place

Organic farming: producing food using manure, compost and natural methods of weed, pest and disease control rather than chemicals

Revision tip

Produce some revision cards or a table to show the advantages and disadvantages of the different types of food production:
- Intensive
- Organic
- Hunting and gathering

ACTIVITY 10.1

Using your knowledge of food provenance, complete the following table. An example has been given to help you:

Animal and plant food production methods	Type of food provenance shown in the picture	Points to consider both positive and negative, about this type of food provenance
	• Free range farming • Organic egg production	• The hens have space and freedom to move around, peck the ground and live naturally • There is less chance of diseases being spread between the hens because they are outside and not all together in one place • The hens will be given organic food to eat • The hens will not be given drugs, antibiotics or other medicines • The cost of land is expensive to keep hens in this way • Natural predators, e.g. foxes can be a problem
	• Intensive chicken meat production	
	• Intensive crop (plant) production	
	• Intensive fish farming	
	• Organic mixed crop (plants) production	
	• Hydroponic plant production (plants grown in water with nutrients added) in a poly-tunnel	

2 Genetically modified (GM) food

- Plants and animals used for food production have unique characteristics, e.g. colour, shape, size, flavour

- These characteristics are passed on by genes to the next generation during reproduction

- Genetic modification (GM) is a complex scientific technique that changes one or more characteristics to make a food have, e.g., a more intense flavour/colour, extra vitamins, etc.

- It is mainly used for plant crops, but there is lots of research currently being carried out on GM animals

- Any ingredients that have been genetically modified must be clearly labelled on food products

The flow chart below shows an example of what happens to produce a new GM food.

Example: Small hot chilli peppers are usually green or red in colour. Some food technologists want to develop a purple coloured small hot chilli pepper using GM technology. This is what they would do:

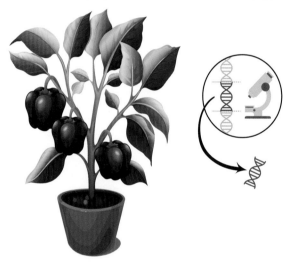

1.
In a laboratory, the biological 'code' in a gene for the colour purple is copied from a purple sweet bell pepper plant.

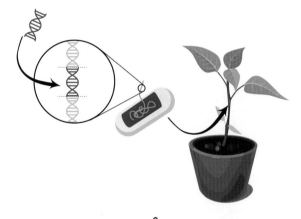

2.
The code is put into a small red chilli pepper plant.

3.
The small red chilli pepper plant produces seeds.

4.
The seeds grow into new plants that will produce small purple chilli peppers.

Some people are in favour of GM food production because:

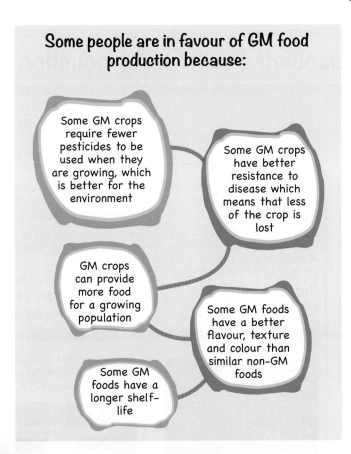

Some GM crops require fewer pesticides to be used when they are growing, which is better for the environment

Some GM crops have better resistance to disease which means that less of the crop is lost

GM crops can provide more food for a growing population

Some GM foods have a better flavour, texture and colour than similar non-GM foods

Some GM foods have a longer shelf-life

Some people are concerned about GM food production because:

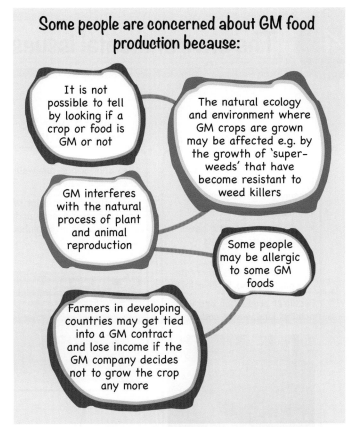

It is not possible to tell by looking if a crop or food is GM or not

The natural ecology and environment where GM crops are grown may be affected e.g. by the growth of 'super-weeds' that have become resistant to weed killers

GM interferes with the natural process of plant and animal reproduction

Some people may be allergic to some GM foods

Farmers in developing countries may get tied into a GM contract and lose income if the GM company decides not to grow the crop any more

3 Seasonal foods

Book-link:
5.1.2 Food and environment, pages 263–268

- Seasonal foods (mainly plants) are ready to be harvested at the stage of their life cycle when they are at their best for flavour, colour and texture

- They are usually cheaper to buy when in season, e.g. strawberries

- Many foods are imported from other parts of the world, and are available all year in UK shops because they grow at different times in other countries

- Importing foods out of season has effects on environmental sustainability, e.g. transporting them uses lots of non-renewable energy (oil) and causes air pollution

- Food imported into the UK can use many food miles and this can impact on climate change

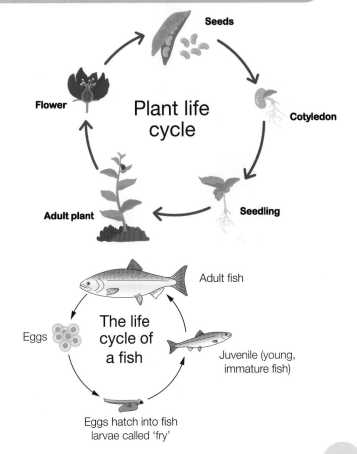

Seeds

Plant life cycle

Flower

Cotyledon

Adult plant

Seedling

Adult fish

The life cycle of a fish

Eggs

Juvenile (young, immature fish)

Eggs hatch into fish larvae called 'fry'

The environmental issues associated with food production

PRODUCTION

Production of meat and dairy foods produces the most greenhouse gases from:

- Fertilisers
- Animals producing gases and waste products
- Intensive farming
- Burning forests to create pasture land for livestock

Fertiliser production and use pollutes land, water and air

PROCESSING & MANUFACTURE

Uses a lot of non-renewable energy and water

Refrigeration uses a lot of non-renewable energy and produces a lot of greenhouse gas emissions

PACKAGING

A lot of plastics and paper are used in food packaging

Many plastics are not biodegradable, i.e. they do not break down and therefore must be disposed of in land fill or by burning, which causes pollution

Plastic production produces greenhouse gases and uses a lot of non-renewable energy (oil). Not all is able to be recycled so causes land and sea pollution

TRANSPORTATION

Many foods and ingredients are transported very long distances – **food miles** – because:

- People drive out of town to shops and restaurants for food
- More food is imported/ exported by air/ship
- Supermarkets transport food by road from distribution centres

Air, sea and land transport uses a lot of non-renewable energy (oil) and causes pollution

All use non-renewable energy (coal, oil) and produce **GREENHOUSE GASES** e.g. CO_2, methane, nitrous oxide

Greenhouse gases trap heat and warm the planet

Higher or lower than normal temperatures

Drought (lack of water)

which causes climate change

Extreme storms

Flooding

Climate change causes:

- Crops fail
- Livestock die
- Soil and nutrients blown or washed away
- Land and farm buildings damaged
- Pollination of crops affected
- Landslides and forest fires cause loss of land, crops and livestock
- Water, soil and land polluted by sewage, rubbish, stones during flooding
- Temperature changes cause insects and moulds to grow in large numbers
- Some plant species die out with climate change

Advantages of buying locally grown foods

The carbon footprint of food

- Measures how much CO_2 and other greenhouse gases are released throughout the production, processing, consumption and disposal of food
- Meat, dairy foods and egg production have the highest carbon footprints
- Vegetable, fruit, nuts, beans and cereal production have the lowest carbon footprints

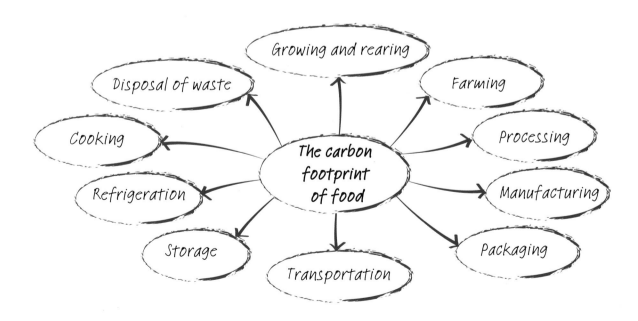

Food waste

- Approximately 7 million tonnes of food is wasted every year in the UK
- Wasted food goes to landfill sites where it rots and gives off a lot of greenhouse gases

The main reasons for wasting food

Consumers:

- Poor meal planning
- Serving portions of food that are too large
- Not storing food properly
- Misunderstanding use-by and best-before dates on food
- Misunderstanding or lack of knowledge about how to store and re-use left-over foods.

Supermarkets and retailers:

- Set rigid standards for the size, shape and appearance of fruits and vegetables
- Any that are misshapen and do not fit the standards for colour and size are thrown away, even though they are edible and nutritious
- There are campaigns to stop this wastage.

Key terms you should try to use in your answers

Greenhouse gases: form an insulating layer around the earth's atmosphere, which traps heat, raises the earth's temperature and causes climate change

Carbon footprint: a measure of the contribution of something (e.g. food production) to the emission of greenhouse gases

Climate change: changes in the earth's temperature that can lead to unusual and extreme weather conditions

Fossil fuels: fuels such as coal, oil and gas that were created over millions of years by fossilised plants and animals

Non-renewable energy: energy produced from fossil fuels that cannot be renewed once they are used up

5 Food security and sustainability

Book-link:
5.1.3 Sustainability of food, pages 269–273

What you must know about food security and sustainability

In your answers, you need to know how to explain the importance of food security and how food production can be made more sustainable

Revision tip

If you have to answer a question about food sustainability, it is a good idea to know an example you could use to show your understanding of the topic, e.g. **sustainable fishing.**

The problems with sea fishing
Damage to habitats and ecology

- Some modern fishing boats (trawlers) drag large nets along the sea bed
- This removes most of the plants and animals (fish and seafood) living there
- It takes years for the ecology of the sea to recover

By-catch

- Many fish are too young/too small to eat so are thrown back (dead) into the sea (called by-catch)
- The sea becomes polluted
- The biodiversity (number of different species of plants and animals) of the sea is reduced

Over-fishing

- The natural fish breeding areas are destroyed
- There is not enough food for the remaining fish to eat because the natural food chain is affected
- Too many fish have been removed from the sea over the last few decades
- There are not enough adult fish left to breed so the fish numbers (stocks) have become seriously reduced

Sustainable solutions

- Conserve the numbers of fish so that they can breed normally
- Limit the number of fish that can be caught by giving fishing boats quotas (maximum amount they can catch)
- Increase the size of holes in fishing nets to allow small fish to escape
- Use sustainable fishing techniques, e.g. line fishing rather than trawlers

---

Food security

Food security means:

- The ability of people to buy enough safe, nutritious and affordable good quality food to meet their own and their family's needs, so they can lead active and healthy lives

Food security is a worldwide problem:

- Many people do not have enough food to eat
- There are fewer resources available to grow food, e.g. land, water, energy, fertile soil

Food security is threatened by:

- Environmental pollution
- Climate change
- Shortage of water
- Economic problems
- Crop failures
- Human activities causing pollution, using water and non-renewable energy, producing greenhouse gases, wasting food, increasing world population

---

Sustainability of food

Food production needs to be sustainable:

- Farmers needs to be paid properly for their hard work and products
- Different varieties of plants and animals need to be protected from disease or becoming extinct
- The welfare of livestock, plants and people in the community who grow the food needs to be protected
- Food production should not damage natural ecosystems (where other plants and animals live)
- Food production should reduce wastage
- Local communities should be encouraged to work together to produce food and protect the environment

---

What consumers can do to produce meals sustainably

- Read food labels carefully – for storage instructions/food provenance
- Buy local foods where possible
- Buy sustainably sourced foods such as fish – check information and logos on food packaging
- Plan carefully to avoid wastage
- Avoid serving too large portions
- Prepare and cook food carefully to avoid wastage
- Use the cooker hob more than the oven – more energy is needed (and wasted) to heat the oven
- If possible, buy Fairtrade food products
- The **Fairtrade foundation** makes sure that farmers and their workers in developing countries receive fair prices for their food products and their labour

ACTIVITY 10.2

Using your knowledge of environmental and sustainability issues around food production, processing and consumption, complete the following table. An example has been given to help you:

Environmental and sustainability issues around food	Environmental and sustainability issue shown in the picture	Points to consider about this issue
	Destruction of the marine (sea) environment by over fishing	Sea fishing is unsustainable because: • Trawler fishing has led to a decrease in fish stocks • The natural ecology of the sea has been damaged • Many fish that are caught are not eaten and thrown back in the sea because they are too young or small • This reduces the number of fish able to breed so the fish stocks decline To make sea fishing more sustainable: • The numbers of fish need to be conserved so that they can breed normally This could be done by: • Limiting the number of fish that can be caught (quotas) • Increasing the size of holes in fishing nets to allow small fish to escape • Using sustainable fishing techniques, e.g. line fishing rather than trawlers • Consumers should buy fish from sustainable sources
	Food wastage	Wasting food is unsustainable because: How to avoid wasting food:

Climate change leading to drought

How is climate change affecting food production?

What can/should be done to slow down climate change?

Fairtrade foods

How is the Fairtrade Foundation helping with food security and sustainability?

Misshapen and undersized vegetables and fruits are often thrown away because supermarkets will not sell them

Why is throwing away misshapen and undersized vegetables and fruits unsustainable?

How can supermarkets and people be encouraged to sell and buy these crops?

The transport of food

Food miles

What are the effects of food miles on the environment?

How can food miles be reduced?

Multiple choice challenge

Have a go at answering these questions. They are worth **one mark** each. Answers are on page 145.

1. **When large numbers of the same type of food crop are grown together in a large field, this is called:**
   a) Invasive farming
   b) Intensive farming
   c) Free range farming
   d) Organic farming

2. **When growing plant crops, organic farming does not allow the use of:**
   a) Manure
   b) Compost
   c) Artificial fertilisers
   d) Tractors

3. **Some plant crops are grown in water that has nutrients added. This type of production is called:**
   a) Hydrophobic
   b) Hydrophilic
   c) Hydroponic
   d) Hydrochloric

4. **The scientific technique that inserts a characteristic from one plant or animal into another to change the colour, flavour or size is called:**
   a) Genetic correction
   b) Organic production
   c) Geographic modification
   d) Genetic modification

5. **When plants are at the stage of their life cycle when they have the best flavour, colour and texture, they are said to be:**
   a) Seasonal
   b) Seasoning
   c) Stale
   d) Seedlings

6. **These are all examples of greenhouse gases:**
   a) Oxygen, methane, nitrous oxide
   b) Carbon dioxide, methane, helium
   c) Oxygen, argon, nitrous oxide
   d) Carbon dioxide, methane, nitrous oxide

7. **Greenhouse gases cause the following to happen:**
   a) Heat escapes from Earth and it cools down
   b) Heat is trapped and Earth heats up
   c) There is no effect on Earth
   d) Heat is trapped but the temperature stays the same on Earth

8. **Food security means:**
   a) Preventing food from being stolen
   b) Storing food safely so that it does not become contaminated
   c) The ability of people to buy enough safe, nutritious and affordable food
   d) The ability of people to buy food that has not been stolen

9. **Food security is threatened by:**
   a) Less land available to grow food
   b) The effects of climate change
   c) Environmental damage
   d) All of these

10. **Producing food in a way that can be maintained over a long period of time and protects the environment is called:**
   a) Fairtrade
   b) Sustainability
   c) Genetic modification
   d) Intensive farming

Knowledge check – can you recall…?

(Answers on page 152)

1. Two methods of food production? *(2 marks)*
2. What organic food production means? *(2 marks)*
3. What hydroponic food production means? *(1 mark)*
4. What intensive farming means? *(2 marks)*
5. Three reasons why people may have concerns about the genetic modification of food? *(3 marks)*
6. Two advantages of eating vegetables when they are in season? *(2 marks)*
7. The production of which types of foods produce the most greenhouse gases? *(2 marks)*
8. Five effects of climate change on food production? *(5 marks)*
9. What food miles means? *(1 mark)*
10. Three advantages of buying locally produced foods? *(3 marks)*

Environmental impact and sustainability

128

Stretch and challenge questions

1. Explain what the term 'food miles' means.   *(1 mark).*

    a) Give two reasons why food miles have increased in recent times.   *(2 marks)*

    b) Give two ways in which food miles have an impact on the environment.   *(2 marks)*

    c) Suggest one way in which food miles can be reduced.   *(1 mark)*

2. Research has shown that in the UK, approximately 20% of the food that consumers buy for their families is thrown away and that most of this wasted food is good enough to eat.

    a) List four reasons why so much food is wasted.   *(4 marks)*

    b) Explain why wasted food has a bad effect on the environment.   *(1 mark)*

    c) How can supermarkets reduce the amount of food waste?   *(4 marks)*

3. In order for there to be food security, food production and consumption need to be sustainable.

    a) Explain what sustainable food production means.   *(5 marks)*

    b) Explain, giving reasons, why the practice of throwing away misshapen and different sized vegetables and fruits because they do not meet the strict standards set by supermarkets, is unsustainable.   *(4 marks)*

    c) Suggest three ways in which consumers could be encouraged to buy and use misshapen and different sized vegetables and fruits.   *(3 marks).*

Chapter 11: Processing and production

What do you need to know?

You now know about where our food comes from and how it is produced.

Next you need to know:

*   The **primary stages** of **food processing**
*   The **secondary stages** of **food processing**
*   How food processing affects the **sensory qualities** and **nutritional properties** of foods
*   How some foods are **nutritionally modified** or **fortified**
*   How **additives** are used in food products

1 Food processing

Book-link:
5.2.1 Food production, pages 274–283

Foods are processed before we eat them for a variety of reasons:

To make foods ready to prepare, cook and serve

To make food safe

To make food appetising and palatable (good to eat)

To make foods appealing and attractive to consumers

Reasons for processing foods

To make foods ready for transportation

To make foods convenient and easy to buy, store and use

To make foods ready for display in shops

There are two main types of food processing:

Primary processing

- This is where foods are processed straight after harvest (plants) or slaughter (animals [livestock])
- Primary processing makes foods ready to use, e.g. wheat grains are turned into flour; meat carcases are cut into separate joints; fish are gutted and either left whole or filleted – heads may be removed
- **Plant foods** (fruits and vegetables) are:
  - sorted (e.g. different sizes)
  - trimmed of leaves and stalks
  - washed – damaged ones are discarded
  - wrapped in packaging
  - prepared for sale by having identification stickers added
  - stored
- **Animal foods** (meat and poultry) after slaughter:
  - blood is drained out
  - skin/feathers are removed
  - internal organs (liver, kidneys, etc.) are removed
  - carcase is hung in a cool place for a few days for enzymes to develop the flavour and tenderise the protein in the muscles
  - carcase/poultry is chilled
  - meat carcase is cut into separate joints ready for cooking, e.g. leg, shoulder, belly, chops
  - poultry is trimmed and trussed (tied up neatly ready for cooking) or cut into joints, e.g. leg quarter, drumstick, thigh, wing, breast

Secondary processing

- This is where primary processed foods are turned into another food product, e.g.:
  - beef turned into minced beef then into burgers
  - whole peaches turned into canned peach slices in fruit juice
  - oranges turned into orange juice or marmalade
  - fish filleted and turned into fish cakes /fish fingers
  - vegetables peeled and chopped and turned into soup
  - chicken meat turned into nuggets or goujons
  - beans /lentils cooked and mixed with other ingredients and turned into vegetarian burgers

Key terms you should try to use in your answers

Primary food processing: when foods are processed straight after harvest or slaughter, to make them ready to be eaten or ready to be used in other food products, such as wheat grain (seeds) turned into flour

Secondary food processing: when primary processed foods are either used on their own or mixed with other foods and turned into other food products, such as wheat flour turned into bread or pasta

Milling: breaking cereal grains (seeds) down and separating the layers, turning the grain into flour

Examples of primary and secondary food processing:

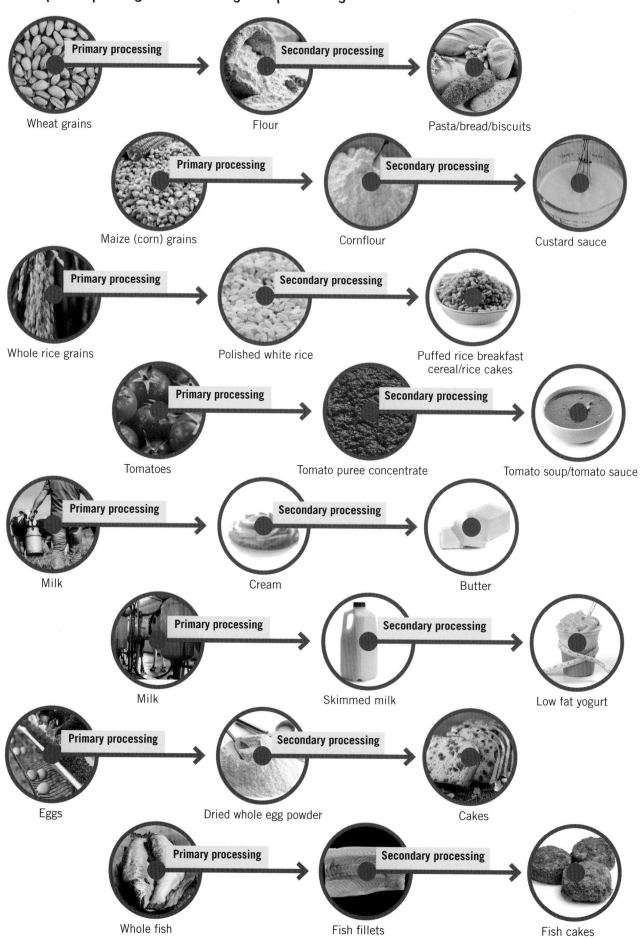

Wheat grains — Primary processing → Flour — Secondary processing → Pasta/bread/biscuits

Maize (corn) grains — Primary processing → Cornflour — Secondary processing → Custard sauce

Whole rice grains — Primary processing → Polished white rice — Secondary processing → Puffed rice breakfast cereal/rice cakes

Tomatoes — Primary processing → Tomato puree concentrate — Secondary processing → Tomato soup/tomato sauce

Milk — Primary processing → Cream — Secondary processing → Butter

Milk — Primary processing → Skimmed milk — Secondary processing → Low fat yogurt

Eggs — Primary processing → Dried whole egg powder — Secondary processing → Cakes

Whole fish — Primary processing → Fish fillets — Secondary processing → Fish cakes

ACTIVITY 11.1

The primary processing of foods often involves several stages.

Primary processing of wheat into flour

a) Label the enlarged drawing of a wheat grain with the different parts and layers:

germ

aleurone layer

endosperm

bran layer

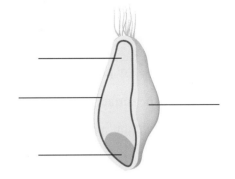

b) Set out below are the stages involved in turning wheat into flour, but they are in the wrong order.

Rearrange the stages into the correct order by numbering them 1 to 4:

☐ Grains are milled to crush them and separate the layers

☐ Grains are cleaned and dried

☐ Grains are harvested

☐ Grains are sieved to produce different types of flour

c) Match the different types of flour with the correct amount of the wheat grain each contains:

wholemeal flour	85%
white flour	100%
wheatmeal (brown) flour	70%

Why is wholemeal flour considered to have the best nutritional profile out of the three types of flour?

Name five different recipes which could be adapted to include the use of wholemeal flour.

Primary processing of milk

a) Milk can have the fat (cream) removed from it by **skimming**.

There are four types of milk available, each with a different fat content, depending on how much was removed by skimming.

Name each of the four milks:

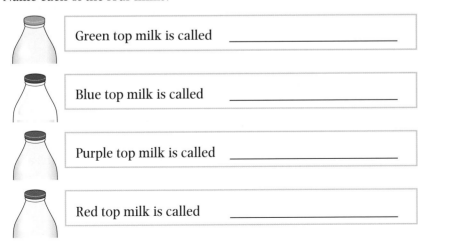

Green top milk is called _____   1% fat

Blue top milk is called _____   0.5–0.9% fat

Purple top milk is called _____   3.9% fat

Red top milk is called _____   1.5–2% fat

Match the different types of milk with the correct amount of fat each contains.

b) Fill in the missing words and temperatures about the next primary stage of processing milk. The missing words are shown below to help you:

Fresh milk is _____ to kill _____ bacteria and make it safe to consume for several

days when stored in the _____ at _____ . Milk is usually _____ during

the first stage of processing. This prevents the _____ from separating from the milk and

rising to the surface. This ensures that the _____ and _____ stay consistent all

the way through. The milk is forced through thousands of tiny _____ under pressure, which

breaks up the _____ and stops it from separating out.

> **Missing words:**
> texture   holes   pathogenic   heat treated   0° and below 5°C
> homogenised   cream   fat   flavour   refrigerator

c) There are three types of heat processing of milk. They involve heating the milk to a specific temperature for a specific amount of time and then rapidly cooling it.

Match the three different types of heat processing of milk with the correct temperature and time they are processed for:

Pasteurisation		110°C for 30 minutes
Ultra Heat Treatment (UHT)		72°C for 15 seconds
Sterilisation		132°C for 1 second

d) Match the three different types of heat treated milk to the correct way in which they are packaged and stored:

Pasteurisation	Stored in sealed bottles (usually made of glass) Can be stored unopened for several months at room temperature Once opened, must be stored in the refrigerator and used within a few days
Ultra Heat Treatment (UHT)	Can be stored in glass or plastic bottles or laminated cartons Must be refrigerated and used within a few days
Sterilisation	Stored in special sealed laminated cartons Can be stored unopened for several months at room temperature Once opened, must be stored in the refrigerator and used within a few days

Explain why milk must be stored in a refrigerator and used within a few days

Here is a revision mind map to help you learn the stages of secondary processing for the production of pasta and yogurt:

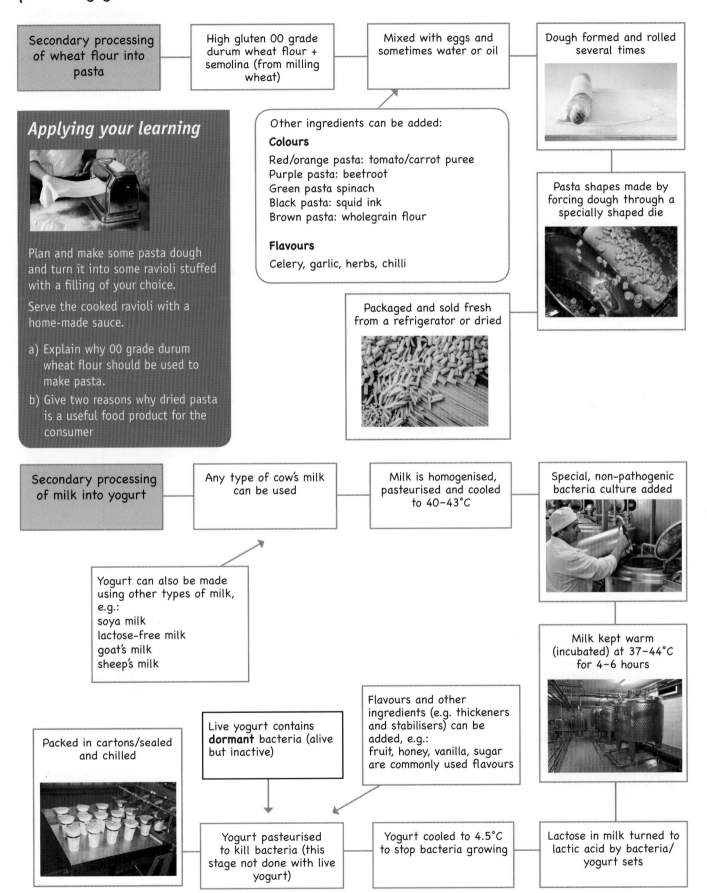

| Secondary processing of wheat flour into pasta | → | High gluten 00 grade durum wheat flour + semolina (from milling wheat) | → | Mixed with eggs and sometimes water or oil | → | Dough formed and rolled several times |

Applying your learning

Plan and make some pasta dough and turn it into some ravioli stuffed with a filling of your choice.

Serve the cooked ravioli with a home-made sauce.

a) Explain why 00 grade durum wheat flour should be used to make pasta.

b) Give two reasons why dried pasta is a useful food product for the consumer

Other ingredients can be added:

Colours
Red/orange pasta: tomato/carrot puree
Purple pasta: beetroot
Green pasta spinach
Black pasta: squid ink
Brown pasta: wholegrain flour

Flavours
Celery, garlic, herbs, chilli

Pasta shapes made by forcing dough through a specially shaped die

Packaged and sold fresh from a refrigerator or dried

Secondary processing of milk into yogurt → Any type of cow's milk can be used → Milk is homogenised, pasteurised and cooled to 40–43°C → Special, non-pathogenic bacteria culture added

Yogurt can also be made using other types of milk, e.g.:
soya milk
lactose-free milk
goat's milk
sheep's milk

Milk kept warm (incubated) at 37–44°C for 4–6 hours

Packed in cartons/sealed and chilled

Live yogurt contains **dormant** bacteria (alive but inactive)

Flavours and other ingredients (e.g. thickeners and stabilisers) can be added, e.g.:
fruit, honey, vanilla, sugar are commonly used flavours

Yogurt pasteurised to kill bacteria (this stage not done with live yogurt)

Yogurt cooled to 4.5°C to stop bacteria growing

Lactose in milk turned to lactic acid by bacteria/ yogurt sets

2 Nutritional modification and fortification

Book-link: 5.2.2 Technological developments associated with better health and food production, pages 284–289

Here is a revision mind map to help you learn about the nutritional modification and fortification of food:

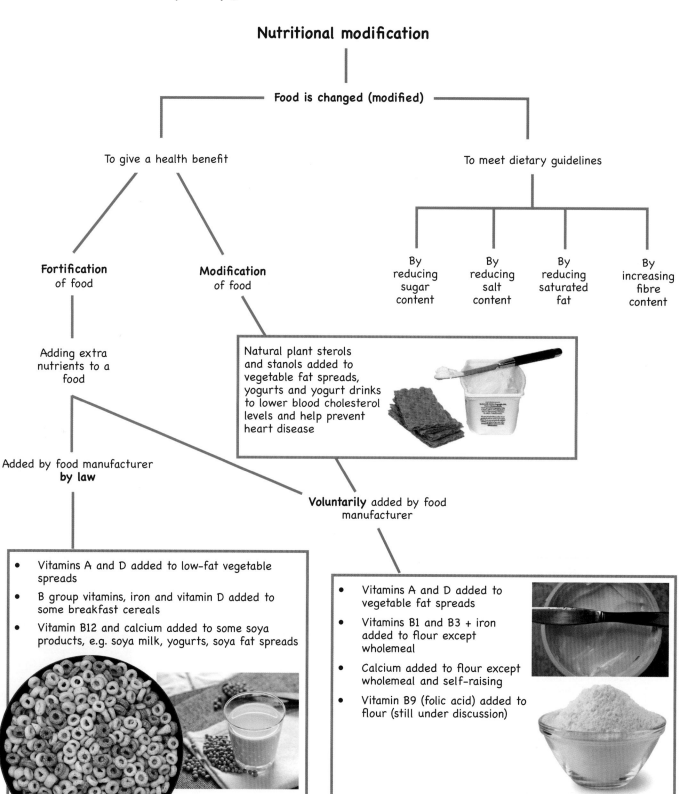

Nutritional modification

Food is changed (modified)

To give a health benefit

To meet dietary guidelines

By reducing sugar content

By reducing salt content

By reducing saturated fat

By increasing fibre content

Fortification of food

Modification of food

Adding extra nutrients to a food

Natural plant sterols and stanols added to vegetable fat spreads, yogurts and yogurt drinks to lower blood cholesterol levels and help prevent heart disease

Added by food manufacturer **by law**

Voluntarily added by food manufacturer

- Vitamins A and D added to low-fat vegetable spreads
- B group vitamins, iron and vitamin D added to some breakfast cereals
- Vitamin B12 and calcium added to some soya products, e.g. soya milk, yogurts, soya fat spreads

- Vitamins A and D added to vegetable fat spreads
- Vitamins B1 and B3 + iron added to flour except wholemeal
- Calcium added to flour except wholemeal and self-raising
- Vitamin B9 (folic acid) added to flour (still under discussion)

3 The use of additives in food products

Food additives are added during manufacture and processing to improve the quality, flavour, colour, texture and stability of foods

The use of additives is controlled by law.

There is concern about how many additives people consume if they eat a lot of processed foods.

Some additives may cause health problems (side effects), e.g. headaches, hyperactivity in children.

Additives (except flavourings) are given E numbers by the European Union (EU).

Foods must be clearly labelled to show which additives they contain.

EMULSIFIERS and STABILISERS are used to improve the structure and texture of foods

Examples:
E322 Lecithins (emulsifiers)
E412 Guar gum

PRESERVATIVES are used to increase the shelf-life of foods

Examples:
E202 Potassium sorbate
E251 Sodium nitrate
Some people are allergic to these additives.

FLAVOURINGS, SWEETENERS, COLOURINGS are used to improve the sensory qualities of foods

Examples of colourings:
E102 Tartrazine
E160b Annatto
Some of these may cause hyperactivity in young children.

Examples of flavourings:
There are thousands.
They do not have E numbers.
Salt is used a lot to flavour foods.

Examples of sweeteners:
E951 Aspartame
E955 Sucralose
Sweeteners may not lower blood sugar levels as much as was once thought.
Some may cause digestive problems, e.g. diarrhoea.

Key terms you should try to use in your answers

Nutritional modification: changing the nutritional profile of a food product so that it meets current dietary guidelines or helps provide a health benefit

Fortification: adding extra nutrients to a food product during its manufacture

Food additives: natural or synthetic (man-made) chemical substances that are added to foods during manufacturing or processing to improve the quality, flavour, colour, texture or stability

Revision tip

You need to know the different *types* of additives and what they are used for.

It is not necessary to learn the different examples of specific additives, e.g. which E number is a particular colouring or preservative, just be aware of E numbers on food labels.

Knowledge check – can you recall...?

(Answers on page 152)

1. The definition of primary processing? *(1 mark)*
2. The definition of secondary processing? *(1 mark)*
3. Four different stages of primary processing for vegetables and fruits? *(4 marks)*
4. The four different parts of a wheat grain? *(4 marks)*
5. The reasons why a meat carcase is hung for a few days after slaughter? *(3 marks)*
6. The reasons why milk is homogenised? *(2 marks)*
7. The reasons why milk is heat treated? *(2 marks)*
8. The four different types of milk available and their colour codes? *(8 marks)*
9. The name of the wheat used to make pasta? *(1 mark)*
10. Two vitamins and two minerals that are added to some foods by law? *(8 marks)*
11. The reasons why emulsifiers and stabilisers are added to some foods? *(2 marks)*
12. Why preservatives are added to some foods? *(1 mark)*
13. What an E number is? *(1 mark)*
14. The possible side effects on children of colourings added to foods? *(1 mark)*
15. Two reasons why nutritional modification is carried out for some food products *(2 marks)*

Stretch and challenge questions

1. Most foods are processed before we eat them.
   a) Give four reasons why foods are processed. *(4 marks)*
   b) Explain what primary processing is and give an example to illustrate your answer. *(2 marks)*
   c) Explain what secondary processing is and give an example to illustrate your answer. *(2 marks)*
2. Cow's milk is consumed in large amounts every day in the UK.
   a) Explain in detail how milk is processed to ensure that it is safe to drink. *(8 marks)*
   b) Explain how milk is processed to give it a consistent texture (same throughout). *(3 marks)*
   c) Explain why a lot of milk is skimmed and what happens during skimming. *(4 marks)*
3. There are many food products available that have been nutritionally modified. Explain, giving examples, what nutritional modification is, why it is done and who might benefit from it. *(12 marks)*
4. In order for there to be food security, food production and consumption need to be sustainable.
   a) Explain what sustainable food production means. *(5 marks)*
   b) Explain, giving reasons, why the practice of throwing away misshapen and different sized vegetables and fruits because they do not meet the strict standards set by supermarkets, is unsustainable. *(4 marks)*
   c) Suggest three ways in which consumers could be encouraged to buy and use misshapen and different sized vegetables and fruits. *(3 marks)*

Multiple choice challenge

Have a go at answering these questions. They are worth **one mark** each. Answers are on page 145.

1. **An example of the primary processing of food is:**
   - a) Milk turned into yogurt
   - b) Flour turned into pasta
   - c) Potatoes sorted into sizes and washed
   - d) Cream turned into butter

2. **An example of the secondary processing of food is:**
   - a) Tomatoes sorted into different sizes
   - b) Meat carcases cut into separate joints
   - c) Milk heat treated
   - d) Fish fillets turned into fishcakes

3. **The colour code for semi skimmed milk is:**
   - a) Green
   - b) Red
   - c) Purple
   - d) Blue

4. **What is removed when milk is skimmed?**
   - a) Protein
   - b) Calcium
   - c) Fat
   - d) Carbohydrate

5. **What does milling mean?**
   - a) Removing the starch from flour
   - b) Breaking cereal grains down to separate the layers
   - c) Harvesting the wheat
   - d) Washing and drying the harvested cereal grains

6. **How much of the cereal grain is used to make wholemeal bread?**
   - a) 60%
   - b) 70%
   - c) 85%

7. **How is milk treated when it is pasteurised?**
   - a) It is heated to 70°C for 12 seconds then rapidly cooled
   - b) It is heated to 72°C for 15 seconds then rapidly cooled
   - c) It is heated to 110°C for 30 minutes then cooled
   - d) It is heated to 132°C for 1 second then rapidly cooled

8. **What is added to milk when making yogurt to make it set?**
   - a) A non-pathogenic bacteria culture
   - b) Lactose
   - c) A pathogenic bacteria culture
   - d) A non-pathogenic mould

9. **Which vitamins are added to vegetable fat spread by law?**
   - a) A and B
   - b) A and C
   - c) B and C
   - d) A and D

10. **Which mineral is added to all types of wheat flour except wholemeal by law?**
    - a) Fluoride
    - b) Zinc
    - c) Iron
    - d) Potassium

Chapter 12: Getting ready for the written examination

Book-link:
Chapter 13, pages 325–334

What do you need to know?

You now know a wide range of information about food preparation and nutrition.

Now you need to know:

- What you will be expected to do in the **written examination**
- How the written examination is organised
- How to be **well prepared and ready** to take the written examination
- The types of questions that you will be asked to answer
- How to follow the **command words** in the examination questions

This chapter will help you get ready for the written examination.

The written examination is worth 50% of your final GCSE grade.

If you are well prepared for it you will be:

 • More relaxed and less nervous

 • More confident about answering questions

 • More likely to be successful and achieve your potential

This is how the exam will be arranged:

Be prepared and ready!

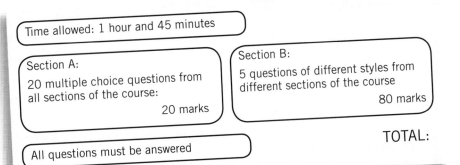

Time allowed: 1 hour and 45 minutes

Section A:
20 multiple choice questions from all sections of the course:
20 marks

Section B:
5 questions of different styles from different sections of the course
80 marks

TOTAL:

All questions must be answered

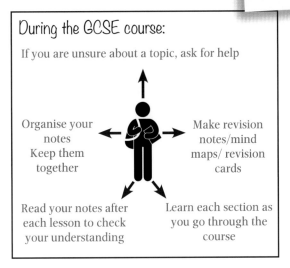

During the GCSE course:

If you are unsure about a topic, ask for help

Organise your notes
Keep them together

Read your notes after each lesson to check your understanding

Make revision notes/mind maps/ revision cards

Learn each section as you go through the course

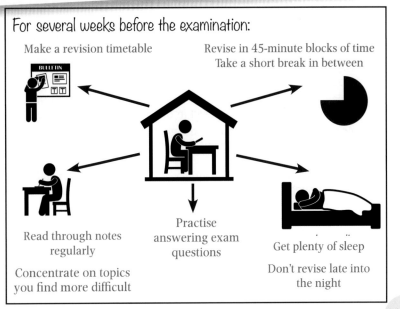

For several weeks before the examination:

Make a revision timetable

Revise in 45-minute blocks of time
Take a short break in between

Read through notes regularly

Concentrate on topics you find more difficult

Practise answering exam questions

Get plenty of sleep

Don't revise late into the night

Revision tip

To help you remember a topic more effectively:

- 'Teach' a topic to a friend or adult and then test each other

- Get someone to ask you questions about a topic

- Cut down the topic into small pieces of information

- Make a visual mind map of a topic using key words/colours/pictures (see the examples throughout this revision guide)

- Make notes with key points/words highlighted

- Make some revision flash cards with key words/definitions on them

- Read the information several times over the weeks before your examination

- Test yourself with practice questions and quizzes on different topics

- Produce a glossary of key words with their meaning

- Produce annotated diagrams to explain some of the scientific elements of the course

ACTIVITY 12.1

Have a go at cutting down the following topic on foams below into small pieces of information.

An example about gluten has been given to help you:

Information to cut down: Gluten	Cut down topic
Consumers expect baked products such as bread and cakes to have a light and open texture. To create the desired texture, a raising agent is added to the uncooked mixture to introduce lots of gas bubbles, which will expand when the mixture is baked in the oven. The mixture itself must have the ability to stretch and rise as the bubbles expand. Baked mixtures are able to stretch and rise because of a protein called **gluten**. Wheat flour contains **gluten**. Gluten is a protein that is formed from two separate proteins called **glutenin** and **gliadin** when **liquid** is added to flour to make a **dough**. When liquid is added to the flour, these proteins mix together to form a **gluten network**. This is usually just called gluten. The dough is kneaded to make it smooth and stretchy. Gluten gives the dough **plasticity**. This means that the dough can be **stretched** and **shaped** during **kneading**. Gluten also makes the dough **elastic**. This means it will shrink back when you stop stretching and shaping it. This is because the long gluten molecules are **coiled**, like the wires on some electrical appliances, and **bend** in different places along their length. As you knead and stretch the dough, the coils and bends straighten out, then when you stop, they relax and gradually go back to their original shape and size. Being able to be stretched and shaped is ideal for **bread making,** because the bread dough needs to be able to stretch when the CO_2 **bubbles** produced by the yeast make the dough expand and **rise**. The gluten network traps the bubbles and then sets when it is baked, thus forming the soft, light texture that you expect inside the bread. WORD COUNT = 287	• Baked foods texture = light and open • Raising agents produce gas bubbles • Bubbles expand in oven → mixture rises • Mixture must able to stretch • Wheat flour contains glutenin & gliadin (proteins) • Water added to flour → glutenin + gliadin form **gluten** → dough formed • Dough kneaded → smooth and stretchy • Gluten gives dough **elasticity** – shrinks back when stretched • Gluten gives dough **plasticity** – can be stretched and shaped • Elasticity and plasticity are ideal for bread dough • Bread dough stretches and rises when CO_2 **bubbles** from yeast **expand** • Gluten network traps bubbles • Gluten sets when baked – gives light open texture WORD COUNT = 94

Now have go at cutting down the following topic on how foams are formed. You could also draw some diagrams to help you to remember it.

Information to cut down: How foams are formed	Cut down topic
The light texture of some foods such as mousses and meringue is produced by creating a **foam**.	
Foams are formed when gases (often air) are trapped inside a liquid to form a **gas-in-liquid foam.**	
Gas (air)-in-liquid foams, are produced when making recipes such as meringue and whisked sponges.	
To make meringue, egg whites are a liquid made of a mixture of proteins and water.	
Egg white is capable of holding up to **7 times** its own volume of air, due to the ability of **egg white protein** to **stretch**.	
When egg whites are whisked to make meringue, the action of the whisk rotating very fast traps lots of air bubbles to make a **gas (air)-in-liquid foam.**	
The action of the whisk also makes some of the compact egg white protein molecules **denature** by breaking the bonds that hold them together and causing them to unfold.	
The denatured protein molecules start joining up and bonding with lots of other denatured protein molecules – this is called **coagulation.**	
They then surround the air bubbles and make a 'wall' around them, which holds the air bubbles and water in place so that the foam is **stabilised.**	
The foam will not form properly if there is any egg yolk, or traces of fat in the mixing bowl.	
If you over-whisk the egg whites, the foam will start to collapse and become watery and loose.	
This is because over-whisking makes the coagulated protein molecules bond together too tightly so that they squeeze out the water they were holding.	
Heating the meringue in the oven coagulates some of the other protein molecules in the egg white and drives some of the water out, so that the foam sets and becomes more solid.	

WORD COUNT = 285

During revision and when all the GCSE examinations start:

- Get plenty of sleep
- Get regular fresh air and exercise
- Drink plenty of water and eat well, including breakfast every day

When you start your written examination:

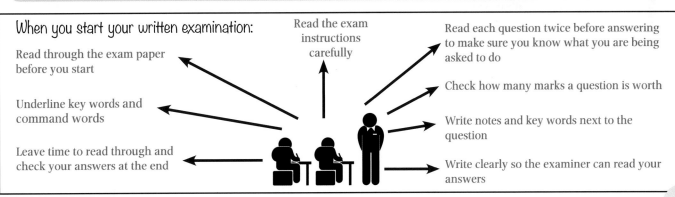

Read the exam instructions carefully

Read through the exam paper before you start

Underline key words and command words

Leave time to read through and check your answers at the end

Read each question twice before answering to make sure you know what you are being asked to do

Check how many marks a question is worth

Write notes and key words next to the question

Write clearly so the examiner can read your answers

Command words

Exam questions are written in different ways using a variety of command words.
Command words tell you what you need to do to answer the question. Make sure that you understand them.

Command word	What it means and what you have to do
Analyse	Break up a topic into different parts and write about them in detail
Comment	Write about a topic and say what you think about it
Compare	Write about the similarities and differences about two or more topics
Consider	Survey some information and write about it giving your views and opinions
Contrast	Identify and write about the differences between two or more topics and say what you think about it
Define	Give a clear and correct meaning of something
Describe	Write in detail about something – e.g. what it is like, what it does, where it come from
Discuss	Write about a topic in a balanced way, e.g. advantages and disadvantages/positive and negative
Evaluate	Write about the importance, value, or quality of a topic, item or activity
Examine	Investigate/consider something and write in detail about what you have found out/concluded
Explain	Write about something in a clear way, giving examples to show your understanding of it
Identify	Show that you understand a topic by giving the important features and points about it
Illustrate	Show your understanding of something by giving suitable examples in your answer
Justify	Say why you think something is better than something else; give some facts to support your answer
Outline	Write about the main parts of a topic
State	Write a short, correct and clear list of facts
Suggest	Write down a list of ideas to solve a problem or manage a situation, e.g. providing suitable food for someone with a health condition
Summarise	Write down the main points about a topic

ACTIVITY 12.2

Look at the questions below in which a variety of different command words have been used. Have a go at answering the questions in the ways in which the command words instruct you to. Try to include examples in your answers:

Questions 1–6 are about fish

1. **Explain** why poaching and steaming are more suitable cooking methods for white fish (e.g. cod, haddock) than grilling. *(5 marks)*
2. **Identify** how the following foods should be stored, giving reasons for your answers:
   a) Frozen prawns that need to be defrosted for use in a meal tomorrow. *(2 marks)*
   b) Fresh haddock bought in the morning for an evening meal. *(2 marks)*
   c) Left-over canned tuna. *(2 marks)*
3. **Compare** the nutritional values of white fish (e.g. cod) and oily fish (e.g. mackerel). *(6 marks)*
4. **Suggest,** with reasons, three ways in which young children could be encouraged to eat fish. *(3 marks)*
5. **State** the quality points to look for when you are buying fresh fish. *(6 marks)*
6. **Discuss** the environmental concerns and sustainability issues around commercial sea fishing. *(10 marks)*

Questions 7–11 are about shortcrust pastry

7. **Describe** why the pastry used for a quiche flan is called 'short crust'. *(4 marks)*
8. **Contrast** the preparation and handling of shortcrust pastry with bread dough in terms of:
   a) The ingredients used. *(3 marks)*
   b) The temperature during the preparation of each. *(2 marks)*
9. **Outline** what happens to the ingredients when shortcrust pastry is baked:
   a) The fat. *(2 marks)*
   b) The flour. *(2 marks)*
   c) The water. *(2 marks)*

10. **Suggest** reasons why shortcrust pastry is a popular food product in many cuisines.
    Illustrate your answer by giving examples. *(6 marks)*

11. **Summarise** why is it not advisable for people to eat a lot of pastry products on a regular basis. *(4 marks)*

Questions 12–16 are about food production and processing

12. a) **Analyse** different methods of egg production. *(4 marks)*

    b) **Explain** how this information will help you to choose which eggs to buy. *(2 marks)*

13. Fairtrade food products are available in most supermarkets in the UK. **Comment** on the importance of the Fairtrade foundation for farmers and workers in developing countries. *(3 marks)*

14. The Scientific Advisory Committee on Nutrition recommends that no more than 5% of daily carbohydrate intake should come from free sugars.
    Consider the reasons why this has been recommended and what people should do to follow the advice. *(5 marks)*

15. **Evaluate** the importance of the following when storing, preparing and cooking food:
    a) Keeping raw and cooked foods separate from each other. *(2 marks)*
    b) To follow 'use-by' and 'best before' dates on food packaging. *(2 marks)*
    c) To chill left-over cooked foods within 1½ –2 hours. *(2 marks)*
    d) To reheat left over foods only once to a minimum core temperature of 75°C for 2 minutes. *(2 marks)*

16. Vegetables can be grown by organic or intensive production methods.
    a) **Contrast** the two production methods. *(4 marks)*
    b) **Justify** which production method is better for environmental sustainability. (2 marks)

Question 17 is about nutrition

17. **Examine** the images on the right:

    Write in detail, giving nutritional facts, about the causes of what has happened in Image A and bone 2 in Image B, and how each condition could be prevented. *(6 marks)*

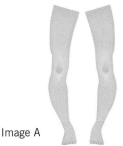

Image A

Bone 1   Bone 2

Image B

Types of questions in the written examination

Section A

In this section, there are 20 multiple choice questions (MCQs), each of which has only one correct answer.

To be successful in answering MCQs you need to read the questions carefully to make sure you understand exactly what is being asked.

In each question there is always:

• **One** correct answer

• **Three** distractors (incorrect) answers

The distractors can be very close to the correct answer so read each question twice through carefully before answering.

ACTIVITY 12.3

Here are three multiple choice questions where the distractor answers are close/similar to the correct answer. Find the correct answer for each one.

1. **Invisible plant oils are found in these foods:**
   - [ ] a) Avocado pears, pumpkin flesh, walnuts, potato crisps
   - [ ] b) Avocado pears, pumpkin seeds, walnuts, potato crisps
   - [ ] c) Pears, pumpkin seeds, walnuts, potato crisps
   - [ ] d) Avocado pears, pumpkin seeds, walnuts, potatoes

2. **Eating too much salt in the diet can cause:**
   - [ ] a) Hyperventilation
   - [ ] b) Hyperactivity
   - [ ] c) Hypertension
   - [ ] d) Hyperlinks

3. **When heat is transferred by the action of atoms vibrating and passing heat energy onto other atoms, it is called:**
   - [ ] a) Coagulation
   - [ ] b) Convection
   - [ ] c) Concentration
   - [ ] d) Conduction

Section B

In this section, the questions are mainly open-ended – they cannot be answered with just a 'yes' or 'no'. Information is needed from you to show your knowledge and understanding of a topic by writing about it in the way that the command words tell you.

There are several styles of open-ended questions:

Data response questions – where you are asked questions about a piece of data you are given, e.g. a food label, a recipe, a chart. Often some extra questions related to the data are asked.

Structured questions – where you are asked questions about a topic and you have to give specific, factual information, e.g. a list, a detailed explanation, examples, a description, a menu for a particular need

Free response questions – where you are given a question about a specific topic and you have to plan how you are going to answer it, including factual information that is relevant to the question.

Advice on answering open-ended questions:

- Read the questions carefully and at least twice so you know what to do
- Make a note of the number of marks being awarded for each question as this gives you an idea of the amount of detail required in the answer
- Study any data you are given very carefully
- Be careful to avoid repeating information in your answers, especially in free response questions
- Do not waste time writing out the question in the answer – this can take up valuable space
- Try to use key terms, e.g. coagulation, contamination, sustainability, when answering questions
- Use proper and complete sentences to communicate your answers clearly to the examiner, except where you are asked for one-word answers or lists
- Write clearly and pay attention to using correct spelling, punctuation and grammar
- Where appropriate, show your knowledge of all aspects of food by including information from different areas of the course in your answers
- Try to provide examples to explain a particular point

ACTIVITY 12.4

Here are a variety of open-ended questions.

Identify which type of open-ended question each is and have a go at answering them.

1. **Yogurt is a very popular dairy product in many countries.**
    a) Suggest two flavourings that can be added to yogurt. *(2 marks)*
    b) Explain why bacteria are added to milk during the production of yogurt. *(2 marks)*
    c) What does 'live yogurt' mean? *(2 marks)*
    d) Explain why yogurt should be stored in refrigerator at 0°C to below 5°C. *(2 marks)*

2. **Many people are choosing to eat a vegetarian diet.**
    Discuss the reasons why a vegan diet may be considered by many people to be:

    Healthier. *(4 marks)*
    More environmentally sustainable. *(4 marks)*
    Consider what advice you would give to a teenager who is considering changing to a vegan diet. *(4 marks)*

3. **Ingredients used in recipes have different functional properties.**
    Explain in detail the functional properties of each ingredient in the recipe for a chocolate sponge cake:

    Self-raising flour *(2 marks)*
    Cocoa powder *(1 mark)*
    Vegetable fat spread *(2 marks)*
    Caster sugar *(2 marks)*
    Eggs *(2 marks)*

4. **Examine the food label on the right, then answer the questions about it:**
    a) State two pieces of information that are required to be shown on a food label by law. *(2 marks)*
    b) How many grams of sugar are there in two biscuits? *(1 mark)*
    c) What is the percentage of saturated fats in the biscuits? *(1 mark)*
    d) Is the fat in the biscuits visible or invisible? Give a reason for your answer. *(2 marks)*
    e) Name two types of food additive in the biscuits. *(2 marks)*
    f) State two reasons why storage instructions are given on the labels of food products. *(2 marks)*
    g) Explain why the manufacturer recommends the following for the biscuits: 'Store in an airtight container once opened.' *(1 mark)*

Choc Oaties

A chocolate-flavoured shortbread and oat biscuit with chocolate chips.

Ingredients: Wheat flour, butter, sugar, rolled oats, chocolate chips (milk, sugar, cocoa butter, cocoa, emulsifiers, flavourings), salt, vanilla flavouring, preservatives (antioxidants)

Allergy information: contains gluten and milk

Storage instructions: Store in an airtight container once opened

Best before end of: December 2017

Net weight: 400g

Made in the UK by Tea Time Foods Ltd., 55, Any Street, London, England

Nutritional Information

Nutrient	Per 100g	Per biscuit (40g)
Energy	2070 kJ / 495 kcals	828 kJ / 198 kcals
Fat – of which:	22.5g	9g
Saturates	12g	4.8g
Carbohydrate – of which:	58.5g	23.4g
Sugars	25g	10g
Starch	33.5g	13.4g
Fibre	2g	0.8g
Protein	15g	6g
Salt	2g	0.8g

Answers

Multiple choice questions

Chapter 1

Q	A	Q	A	Q	A
1	D	11	A	21	C
2	B	12	B	22	B
3	C	13	D	23	A
4	A	14	A	24	A
5	C	15	C	25	C
6	B	16	B	26	B
7	C	17	A	27	C
8	C	18	C	28	B
9	C	19	A	29	A
10	B	20	D	30	D

Chapter 2

Q	A	Q	A
1	B	11	B
2	C	12	B
3	D	13	C
4	B	14	B
5	D	15	D
6	C	16	B
7	D	17	C
8	A	18	B
9	B	19	C
10	D	20	B

Chapter 3

Q	A
1	B
2	C
3	B
4	D
5	A
6	C
7	A
8	D
9	B
10	C

Chapter 4

Q	A	Q	A
1	B	11	A
2	D	12	D
3	A	13	D
4	C	14	B
5	A	15	C
6	B	16	A
7	D	17	D
8	C	18	B
9	C	19	C
10	C	20	B

Chapter 5

Q	A	Q	A
1	C	11	A
2	D	12	B
3	B		
4	D		
5	A		
6	B		
7	C		
8	D		
9	A		
10	D		

Chapter 6

Q	A	Q	A
1	C	11	D
2	B	12	C
3	D	13	B
4	A	14	B
5	B	15	D
6	A		
7	B		
8	B		
9	A		
10	C		

Chapter 7

Q	A
1	B
2	A
3	C
4	A
5	C
6	B
7	C
8	C
9	A
10	C

Chapter 8

Q	A
1	D
2	B
3	C
4	D
5	C
6	B
7	D
8	C
9	D
10	C

Chapter 9

Q	A
1	B
2	D
3	C
4	B
5	C
6	B
7	D
8	B
9	C
10	A

Chapter 10

Q	A
1	B
2	C
3	C
4	D
5	A
6	D
7	B
8	C
9	D
10	B

Chapter 11

Q	A
1	C
2	D
3	A
4	C
5	B
6	D
7	B
8	A
9	D
10	C

Knowledge check – Can you recall...?

NOTE: This section contains suggested model answers that would achieve a good mark if you gave them in an exam. They are designed to help guide and instruct you, but they <u>should not</u> be considered to be the only answers you could give.

Chapter 1

1. What protein complementation means? *(1 mark)*

    Eating a mixture of LBV proteins together to get all the essential amino acids

2. What amino acids are? *(1 mark)*
    - The building blocks of protein molecules

3. The functions of protein in the body? *(3 marks)*
    - Body growth
    - Repair of body
    - Source of energy

4. Five foods that contain HBV proteins? *(5 marks)*

    Milk, cheese, yogurt, eggs, fish, chicken, meat, quinoa, soya beans

5. Five foods that contain LBV proteins? *(5 marks)*

    Peas, beans, lentils, gelatine, cereal grains, seeds

6. Three things that happen to people if they don't have enough protein? *(3 marks)*
    - Children do not grow properly
    - They may lose some hair
    - Skin and nails will be in poor condition
    - They will develop infections
    - They will not be able to digest food properly

7. What the name of a fat molecule is? *(1 mark)*
    Triglyceride

8. The functions of fat in the body? *(4 marks)*
    - Store of energy
    - Insulates body from the cold to keep it warm
    - Protects bones and kidneys from damage with a cushion of fat
    - Gives the body vitamins A, D, E, and K

9. What a fatty acid is? *(1 mark)*
    Part of the triglyceride molecule

10. Four foods that contain mainly saturated fatty acids? *(4 marks)*
    Butter, lard, suet, block vegetable fat, ghee, meat fat, palm oil, coconut, chocolate

11. Four foods that contain mainly unsaturated fatty acids? *(4 marks)*
    Plants oils: olive, rapeseed, sunflower, corn; oily fish; avocado pears, nuts, seeds, some vegetable fat spreads

12. Why fatty foods are energy dense? *(1 mark)*
    They provide 9 kcals/37 kJ per gram (more than carbohydrates and protein)

13. Why cakes, pastries, biscuits, crisps, etc., contain invisible fat? *(1 mark)*
    The fat melts and is absorbed into the mixture during baking

14. Two health conditions that people might get if they eat too much fat? *(2 marks)*
    - Obesity
    - Coronary heart disease

15. The functions of carbohydrate in the body? *(2 marks)*
    - Main source of energy in the diet
    - Provides dietary fibre to get rid of waste products and prevent constipation

16. The two main groups of carbohydrates? *(2 marks)*
    - Sugars
    - Complex carbohydrates

17. The names of the three monosaccharides? *(3 marks)*
    Glucose, galactose, fructose

18. The names of the three disaccharides? *(3 marks)*
    Sucrose, maltose, lactose

19. The names of the four polysaccharides found in foods? *(4 marks)*
    Starch, dietary fibre (non-starch polysaccharide [NSP]), pectin, dextrin

20. The name of the polysaccharide made by animals and humans in their bodies? *(1 mark)*
    Glycogen

21. Two health conditions that people might get if they eat too much carbohydrate? *(2 marks)*
    - Type 2 diabetes
    - Obesity
    - Tooth decay

22. What free sugars are and why they should be limited in the diet? *(2 marks)*
    Sugars released during food processing or added to foods by manufacturers, cooks and consumers, e.g. honey, sugar [sucrose], syrups, fruit juices

23. Which vitamins are fat soluble? *(4 marks)*
    A, D, E, K

24. Which vitamins help energy to be released from food in the body? *(3 marks)*
    B1, B2, B3

25. Which vitamin helps the body absorb iron? *(1 mark)*
    Vitamin C

26. Which vitamin helps the body absorb calcium? *(1 mark)*
    Vitamin D

27. Which three vitamins are antioxidants? *(3 marks)*
    A, C, E

28. Which vitamin is made in the body from the action of sunlight on the skin? *(1 mark)*
    Vitamin D

29. Which two vitamins help the body to make healthy red blood cells? *(2 marks)*
    Vitamins B9 and B12

30. Which mineral causes high blood pressure if you have too much of it in food? *(1 mark)*
    Sodium

31. The name of the deficiency disease caused by not enough vitamin C? *(1 mark)*
    Scurvy

32. The name of the deficiency disease in children caused by not enough vitamin D? *(1 mark)*
    Rickets

33. The name of the deficiency disease in adults caused by not enough vitamin D? *(1 mark)*
    Osteomalacia

34. The name of the deficiency disease caused by not enough vitamin A? *(1 mark)*
    Night blindness

35. The name of the deficiency disease caused by not enough vitamin B1? *(1 mark)*
    Beri-beri

36. The name of the deficiency disease caused by not enough vitamin B12? *(1 mark)*
    Pernicious anaemia

37. The function of vitamin K in the body? *(1 mark)*

    To help the blood to clot when the body is injured

38. The name of the deficiency disease caused by not enough iron? *(1 mark)*
    Iron deficiency anaemia

39. Five reasons why the body needs water? *(5 marks)*
    - For all cells, tissues and fluids [blood, urine, sweat, digestive juices]
    - Chemical reactions in body use water
    - Body temperature controlled by removing heat by sweating
    - For digestion of food and absorption of nutrients
    - Removes waste products from body
    - Mucous membranes are kept moist
    - Controls concentrations of substances in the blood
    - Keeps skin moist and healthy

40. Three symptoms of being dehydrated? *(3 marks)*
    - Thirst
    - Headache
    - Urine dark in colour
    - Feeling weak and sick
    - Body overheats
    - Wrinkled skin
    - Confusion
    - Changes in blood pressure and heart rate

Chapter 2

1. The eight dietary guidelines? *(8 marks)*
   1. Base your meals on starchy foods
   2. Eat lots of fruit and vegetables
   3. Eat more fish, including oily fish
   4. Cut down on saturated fat and sugar
   5. Eat less salt – no more than 6g day (for adults)
   6. Get active and be a healthy weight
   7. Don't get thirsty – drink plenty of water
   8. Don't skip breakfast

2. What the word 'diet' means? *(1 mark)*
   The food that you eat every day

3. The names of five special diets? *(5 marks)*
   - Weight reduction/calorie controlled
   - Low fat
   - Low salt
   - Low sugar
   - High fibre
   - Vegetarian
   - Coeliac
   - Diabetic

4. What a healthy balanced diet means? *(1 mark)*
   A diet that contains the correct proportions of nutrients and water necessary for good health, to grow properly, be active and maintain a healthy weight

5. Five general rules for planning meals for anyone? *(5 marks)*
   Take into account:
   - Peoples' likes and dislikes
   - Everyday meal or special occasion?
   - Food allergies and intolerances
   - Religious or culinary dietary rules
   - Nutritional profile of a meal
   - Health conditions
   - People's lifestyle
   - Time available to prepare and cook food
   - Cost of ingredients
   - Availability of foods/seasonality

6. Three best eating habits and lifestyle choices for children aged 1–4 years? *(3 marks)*
   - Small regular meals
   - Try new foods
   - Eat fresh and raw foods
   - Drink unsweetened drinks – especially water and whole milk
   - Eat until full
   - Sit at a table to eat if possible
   - Share and enjoy food with others
   - Don't eat snacks between meals
   - Avoid high fat, high sat, high sugar snacks

7. Three best eating habits and lifestyle choices for children aged 5–12 years? *(3 marks)*
   - Follow Eatwell guide and dietary guidelines
   - Try new foods regularly
   - Eat plenty of fresh foods
   - Eat regular meals, especially breakfast
   - Take part in food purchase, choice, preparation and cooking
   - Avoid 'grazing' on food during the day
   - Avoid frequently eating sweet, fatty and salty snack foods in between meals

8. Three best eating habits and lifestyle choices for teenagers? *(3 marks)*
   - Follow Eatwell guide and dietary guidelines
   - Try new foods regularly
   - Eat plenty of fresh foods
   - Eat regular well-balanced meals, especially breakfast
   - Take part in food purchase, choice, preparation and cooking
   - Avoid 'grazing' on food during the day
   - Avoid frequently eating sweet, fatty and salty snack foods in between meals
   - Avoid missing meals

9. Three best eating habits and lifestyle choices for adults? *(3 marks)*
   - Follow Eatwell guide and dietary guidelines
   - Eat plenty of fresh foods
   - Eat regular well-balanced meals, especially breakfast
   - Take part in food purchase, choice, preparation and cooking
   - Avoid 'grazing' on food during the day
   - Avoid frequently eating sweet, fatty and salty snack foods in between meals
   - Avoid missing meals

10. Three best eating habits and lifestyle choices for elderly adults? *(3 marks)*
    - Follow Eatwell guide and dietary guidelines
    - Eat plenty of fresh foods
    - Eat small, regular, well-balanced meals, especially breakfast
    - Avoid eating too many energy dense foods
    - Avoid adding lots of salt and free sugars to foods and drinks
    - Avoid missing meals

11. Why iron and vitamin C are especially important for teenage girls and adult women? *(1 mark)*
    - Menstruation can result in iron deficiency anaemia
    - Iron rich foods will help to make up losses of iron
    - Vitamin C needed to absorb the iron from food

12. Why calcium and vitamin D are especially important for teenagers and adults? *(2 marks)*
    Skeleton is strengthening as minerals are laid down in it
    Need calcium for peak bone mass and vitamin D to absorb calcium in the body

13. Why protein is especially important for young children? *(1 mark)*
    For growth

14. Why vitamins A, C and E are especially important for elderly adults? *(1 mark)*
    These are antioxidants and help to prevent heart disease and cancer

15. Two foods that lacto vegetarians do eat and two that they do not? *(4 marks)*
    Do eat: milk, cheese, yogurt, cream, fruits, butter, vegetables, cereals
    Do not eat: eggs, meat, fish, poultry

16. Two foods that a coeliac can eat and two that they cannot? *(4 marks)*
    Can eat: almonds, buckwheat, cassava, corn (maize), linseeds, millet, polenta, peas, beans, lentils, quinoa, rice, soya flour
    Cannot eat: wheat, barley, oats, rye

17. Two foods that someone on a low sodium diet can eat and two that they should not? *(4 marks)*
    Can eat: fruits, vegetables, peas, beans, lentils, poultry, milk, natural yogurt, unsalted butter
    Should not eat: ham, bacon, cured meats e.g. chorizo, cheese, yeast extract (e.g. Marmite), soy sauce, some processed foods, e.g. dips, salad dressings, ready meals, sauces, soups, fried snacks, roasted nuts

18. Three reasons why the body needs energy? *(3 marks)*
    - To move muscles and be active
    - To make body heat
    - To make sound
    - To make the nerves work and send messages from the brain
    - For chemical reactions in the body
    - To make the body grow and develop

19. What an energy dense food is? *(1 mark)*
    One that contains a lot of fat and/or carbohydrate and has a high energy value

20. The main source of energy for the body? *(1 mark)*
    Carbohydrates

21. What happens to the body if you have excess energy from food? *(1 mark)*
    Weight gain leading to obesity

22. What BMR means and what its definition is? *(2 marks)*
    Basal Metabolic Rate – amount of energy needed to keep the body alive

23. Two reasons why physical activity is important for the body? *(2 marks)*
    - Reduces risk of developing diseases such as heart disease, obesity, some cancers
    - For the health of the skeleton and muscles
    - Keeps brain alert
    - For feeling good

24. Three possible effects on the body of being obese? *(3 marks)*
    - Large amounts of fat stored under the skin and in the abdomen around the intestines
    - Type 2 diabetes
    - Damage to joints in knees and hips
    - Strain on the heart, blood vessels, liver, kidneys, skeleton and muscles

25. Three possible effects on the body of having Type 2 diabetes? *(3 marks)*
    - Thirst
    - Tiredness and weakness
    - Weight loss
    - Frequent urination
    - Blurred vision
    - Poor eyesight – eventual blindness
    - Numbness in fingers and toes
    - Skin will not heal properly

26. Three possible effects on the body of having high blood pressure? *(3 marks)*
    - Developing coronary heart disease
    - Stroke (blood clot in brain)
    - Damage to eyes and kidneys

27. Three risk factors that may lead to the development of coronary heart disease? *(3 marks)*
    - High intake of saturated fats
    - High intake of salt
    - Stress
    - Obesity
    - Smoking
    - Lack of exercise
    - Alcohol
    - Family history of CHD
    - High blood pressure

28. How tooth decay develops? *(3 marks)*
    - Mouth contains many bacteria
    - Bacteria feed on food residues on teeth (plaque)
    - Sugars and starches turned into acids by bacteria
    - Acids dissolve enamel coating on teeth
    - Hole develops in tooth and bacteria infect it

29. Two types of foods/drinks to avoid in order to prevent tooth decay? *(2 marks)*
    - Sugary foods
    - Foods with processed/refined carbohydrates (starch)
    - Sweetened soft drinks
    - Concentrated fruit juices

30. Three symptoms of iron deficiency anaemia? *(3 marks)*
    - Tiredness
    - Weakness
    - Lack of energy
    - Pale inner eye lids
    - Pale complexion
    - Weak, ridged finger nails
    - Feeling cold

Chapter 3

1. What electro-magnetic waves in microwaving do? *(1 mark)*
   Vibrate water molecules which transfers heat energy

2. The names of the cooking methods where dry heat is used to transfer heat energy to food? *(4 marks)*
   Baking, grilling/barbequing, toasting, dry frying

3. The names of the cooking methods where oil is used to transfer heat energy to food? *(5 marks)*
   Sautéing, shallow frying, deep fat frying, roasting, stir frying

4. The names of the cooking methods where moisture is used to transfer heat energy to food? *(6 marks)*
   Boiling, braising, poaching, simmering, steaming, stewing

5. Five foods that are suitable to be cooked by moist cooking methods? *(5 marks)*
   Meat, poultry, vegetables, rice, fish, eggs, bacon, peas, beans, lentils, etc.

6. Three foods that are suitable to be cooked by dry heat methods? *(3 marks)*
   Cakes, biscuits, breads, pastries, meat, poultry, scones, fish, etc.

7. What happens to starch when it is heated in moisture? *(2 marks)*
   It absorbs water and gelatinises between 60°C and 100°C

8. What happens to minced beef when it is cooked by dry frying? *(2 marks)*
   Fat melts, proteins denature and coagulate, juices squeezed out of meat (flavour develops), meat changes from red to brown colour

9. What happens to meat or fish if they are cooked for too long under a grill? *(2 marks)*
   The protein denatures and coagulates and squeezes out moisture, which makes them dry, tough and less digestible

10. Four ways of conserving the vitamins in vegetables? *(4 marks)*
    - Choose fruits and vegetables that are very fresh and undamaged
    - Cut and prepare just before cooking or serving raw
    - Cook in only a little water for the shortest time possible
    - Use cooking water for soups or gravies
    - Serve straight away

11. Why gas and ordinary electric ovens have zones of heat? *(2 marks)*
    - Heat rises by convection
    - Top shelf will be the hottest
    - As convection currents start to fall they cool
    - Middle shelf will be approximately at the set oven temperature
    - Bottom shelf will be the coolest

12. Why foods can be baked evenly on any shelf in an electric fan oven? *(2 marks)*
    The fan distributes the heat evenly in the oven so there are no zones of heat

13. Why microwaving heats food very quickly? *(2 marks)*
    Microwaves go into the food and make water molecules vibrate very fast. Vibrations cause heat energy to be passed very quickly into food molecules which rapidly heat up

14. Why cakes, pastries, biscuits, scones, etc., develop a golden brown crust when baked in the oven? *(2 mark)*
    The dry heat in the oven changes the starch molecules into smaller groups of glucose molecules called dextrin. This changes the colour to a golden brown. The process is called dextrinisation.

15. Why stir frying is considered to be a healthier method of cooking than shallow frying? *(1 mark)*
    Very little oil is used to cook the foods, so they have low energy density. The foods are stir fried for a short time so less damage is done to the vitamins they contain

Chapter 4

1. The chemical structure of protein molecules? *(2 marks)*
   Large molecules made up of units called amino acids. The molecules are folded into bundles and held together by chemical bonds

2. What the word 'denaturation' means? *(1 mark)*
   The chemical bonds in the protein molecules are broken so the molecule opens up and changes shape

3. What the word 'coagulation' means? *(1 mark)*
   Denatured protein molecules start to join up with others in large groups

4. Three reasons why gluten is important in baked products? *(3 marks)*
   - Gluten gives doughs plasticity so they can be stretched and shaped during kneading
   - Gluten makes dough elastic so it can rise when baked
   - Gluten network traps bubbles of gas in doughs and sets when baked to give a light texture

5. How foams are formed using egg whites? *(2 marks)*
   - Egg white protein can stretch when whisked and hold seven times its own volume of air
   - Whisking traps air to form a gas-in-liquid foam
   - Denatured egg white proteins coagulate and form a wall around the air bubbles to stabilise them

6. What happens to starch when it is heated with a liquid? *(4 marks)*
   - Starch granules sink to the bottom of a pan in cold water
   - They start to absorb water at 60°C and swell
   - At 80°C they are very swollen and start to burst and release starch molecules
   - Starch molecules start to form a 3D network trapping water molecules
   - At 100°C the starch molecules completely thicken the liquid
   - Whole process = gelatinisation

7. What happens to starch when it is heated under a grill or in an oven? *(2 marks)*
   - Dry heat causes the starch molecules to break into smaller group of glucose molecules called dextrin

- Food product develops a golden brown colour on the outside and a toasted flavour
- Whole process = dextrinisation

8. What caramelisation means? *(1 mark)*
   - Heating sugar (sucrose) causes it to turn into a syrup
   - As heating continues, the hydrogen and oxygen molecules it contains form water, which evaporates
   - The colour of the sugar syrup changes to golden brown as it caramelises

9. What gelatinisation means? *(1 mark)*
   The swelling of starch granules when they are cooked with a liquid to the point where they burst and release starch molecules

10. What dextrinisation means? *(1 mark)*
    The breaking up of starch molecules into smaller groups of glucose molecules when they are exposed to dry heat

11. The chemical structure of fat molecules? *(2 marks)*
    - One molecule =
    - 1 unit of glycerol with 3 fatty acids attached
    - Called a triglyceride

12. What plasticity means? *(1 mark)*
    The ability of a fat to soften over a range of temperatures and be shaped and spread with light pressure

13. What shortening means? *(1 mark)*
    The ability of fats to shorten the length of gluten molecules in pastry

14. How fats aerate a mixture? *(2 marks)*
    - Some fats can trap lots of air bubbles when beaten together with sugar – called 'creaming'
    - Each air bubble is surrounded by a thin layer of fat and a foam is created

15. How oil and water are emulsified? *(3 marks)*
    - Oil and water will not mix together – they separate
    - They can be prevented from separating by an emulsifier, e.g. lecithin in egg yolk
    - Emulsifier molecule has one end that 'like' water (hydrophilic) and one end that 'dislikes' water (hydrophobic)
    - When added to oil and water, the emulsifier molecules arrange themselves to prevent the oil and water from separating
    - The mixture becomes an emulsion

16. Four ways in which air can be trapped in a mixture? *(4 marks)*
    Sieving flour, creaming, whisking, rolling and folding and rolling pastry

17. Two ways in which carbon dioxide gas can be introduced into a mixture? *(2 marks)*
    - Adding baking powder (bicarbonate of soda)
    - Adding yeast

18. How gases from raising agents make a baked mixture rise? *(2 marks)*
    - Gases expand with heat
    - As they expand they push baked mixtures upwards and outwards until the mixture sets

19. The four conditions yeast needs to be able to produce carbon dioxide gas? *(4 marks)*
    Warmth, moisture, sugar/starch, time

20. Why the oven must be very hot in order for batters (*e.g.* Yorkshire puddings) and choux pastry to rise? *(2 marks)*
    - They both contain a lot of water
    - When heated to 100°C+ the water turns to steam
    - The steam raises the mixture
    - Steam will not form quickly enough if the oven temperature is not hot enough

Chapter 5

1. What food spoilage means? *(1 mark)*
   Something has made food unsafe and unfit to eat

2. What enzymes are? *(1 mark)*
   Natural substances (biological catalysts) in living things that speed up chemical reactions

3. The names of the three types of micro-organisms? *(3 marks)*
   Bacteria, moulds, yeasts

4. Five places where you find micro-organisms? *(5 marks)*
   Soil, water, people, animals, pests, e.g. flies and mice, dust, sewage, rubbish, food packaging, air, dirt, surfaces, equipment, clothing, food

5. The five conditions micro-organisms need to grow and multiply? *(5 marks)*
   Suitable temperature, moisture, food supply, enough time, the right pH (acidity/alkalinity)

6. What happens to micro-organisms if the temperature is very cold? *(1 mark)*
   Their growth and multiplication slow down until it stops – they become dormant

7. What happens to micro-organisms if the temperature is very hot? *(1 mark)*
   Most of them are killed

8. The names of the five main types of bacteria that cause food poisoning? *(5 marks)*
   - Campylobacter
   - E.Coli
   - Salmonella
   - Listeria
   - Staphylococcus Aureus

9. What pathogenic means? *(1 mark)*
   A micro-organism that is harmful to humans and causes food poisoning

10. What high risk foods are and give three examples of them? *(4 marks)*
    - Foods that contain a lot of moisture and nutrients, especially protein.
    - Milk, cream, eggs, meat, fish, poultry

11. What the Danger zone is? *(1 mark)*
    5°C – 63°C – when bacteria multiply rapidly in food

12. Why bacteria spores are particularly dangerous? *(1 mark)*
    - They are not easily destroyed by heat

- They germinate when conditions are right and produce very dangerous toxins (poisons)

13. The four groups of people who should avoid eating high-risk foods such as soft cheeses and undercooked meat and eggs? *(4 marks)*
    - Babies and young children
    - Pregnant women
    - Elderly people
    - People who have a weak immune system

14. Why it is not a good idea to scrape mould off a food and then eat the rest of the food? *(1 mark)*
    - Moulds put down 'roots' (mycelium) into food
    - Waste products containing toxins go out through the roots and into the food
    - If the mould is scraped off the surface, the mycelium and toxins may remain in the food

15. Why do some vegetables and fruits turn brown after a few minutes when you cut them? *(1 mark)*
    - Enzymes are released, which mix with oxygen from the air and substances in the cells
    - This causes the substances in the cells to change colour

16. What fermentation means? *(1 mark)*
    The breakdown of sugar molecules into CO_2 gas and alcohol by yeasts

17. What pasteurisation means? *(1 mark)*
    - Heat treatment to destroy pathogenic bacteria in milk and other foods
    - Milk is heated to 72°C for 15 seconds then rapidly cooled

18. Why lactic acid produced by bacteria in yogurt making makes it change from a liquid to a semi-solid? *(1 mark)*
    The lactic acid denatures and coagulates the protein in the milk which changes its texture

19. When making cheese, which two things milk turns into when rennet is added? *(2 marks)*
    Curds (solids) and whey (liquid)

20. How enzymes change the colour, texture and flavour of unripe bananas? *(3 marks)*
    - Unripe bananas contain starch and are green in colour and have a hard texture
    - The colour changes from green to yellow to brown/black
    - The texture softens and gradually becomes syrupy
    - Enzymes gradually break down the starch molecules into sugars which makes the flavour become sweeter

Chapter 6

1. Three different places where food can be bought? *(3 marks)*
   Supermarkets, covered/street markets, small independent/specialist shops, e.g. butchers, bakers, fishmongers, online home delivery companies, direct from farms, farmers' markets

2. What use-by means? *(1 mark)*
   The date by which high risk foods should be eaten

3. Three examples of food that have use-by dates? *(3 marks)*

E.g. chicken, fresh meat, yogurt, cream, milk, cheese, fresh fish

4. What best-before means? *(1 mark)*

The date after which non-high risk foods will still be safe to eat but will not be at their best quality in terms of flavour, texture, appearance

5. Three examples of food that have best-before dates? *(3 marks)*

E.g. biscuits, breakfast cereal, canned foods, frozen foods

6. What 'tainted' means? *(1 mark)*

When a food picks up the flavour or smell of another food nearby, which spoils its palatability

7. Four pieces of food safety advice to look out for on food packaging? *(4 marks)*

- Storage instructions
- Star rating for storage of food in a freezer
- Heating and cooking instructions
- Defrosting instructions for frozen foods
- Allergy advice
- Shelf-life advice – i.e. use-by and best-before dates

8. Four qualities to look out for when choosing to buy fresh fish? *(4 marks)*

- Bright red gills
- Firm flesh
- Fresh smell
- Clear shiny eyes – not sunken
- Firmly attached scales – not loose
- Moist skin – not slimy

9. Four qualities to look out for when choosing to buy fresh meat? *(4 marks)*

- Not too much fat
- Fresh smell
- Firm, springy texture
- Moist flesh – not wet or slimy
- Bright red/pink colour

10. Four qualities to look out for when choosing to buy fresh fruit? *(4 marks)*

- Good texture – not too soft
- Bright colour
- Undamaged skin
- No mould or yeast growth
- Unwrinkled skin (apart from passionfruit)

11. Three points to remember when storing dried foods? *(3 marks)*

- Store in well-ventilated cupboard
- Protect from pests and dust
- Once opened, seal and store in airtight containers
- Regularly check best before dates
- Use up old stocks of food before new ones

12. Three points to remember when storing refrigerated foods? *(3 marks)*

- Do not allow uncooked foods, e.g. poultry, to drip onto or touch cooked foods
- Place foods such as eggs away from strong smelling foods to avoid them becoming tainted

- Protect foods from moisture loss by covering/wrapping them or storing them in airtight boxes
- Allow air to circulate in the refrigerator – do not overcrowd the shelves
- Make sure temperature of refrigerator is between 0°C and below 5°C

13. Three points to remember when storing frozen foods? *(3 marks)*

- Cover/wrap foods well to avoid them getting freezer burn
- Protect foods from moisture loss and taint from other foods
- Make sure temperature of freezer is between −18°C and −24°C
- Label each food clearly with name of product and date it was frozen
- Use up older foods before newer ones
- Regularly defrost the freezer to make sure it works efficiently

14. Three types of materials that are suitable for food storage? *(3 marks)*

- Plastic boxes, bags and cling film
- Greaseproof and silicon paper
- Glass dishes, jars and other containers
- Ceramic and china dishes
- Aluminium foil and containers, stainless steel containers

15. Ten personal hygiene rules for preparing and cooking food? *(10 marks)*

- Tie back and cover hair
- Do not cough, spit or sneeze over food
- Do not put fingers in your mouth then put them back into the food
- Do not 'double dip' when checking the flavour of food you have made
- Use a clean spoon for taste testing or sensory analysis
- Cover outdoor clothing with clean apron or jacket
- Do not wear jewellery on hands, round neck or in your ears
- Do not allow sweat to drop into food
- Regularly wash and dry hands thoroughly
- Keep fingernails short and clean
- Do not wear nail varnish or false nails
- Do not put feet or shoes on work surfaces where food is prepared

16. Three points to remember when handling raw and cooked foods? *(3 marks)*

- Use different coloured chopping boards
- Use different preparation equipment for each
- Do not allow them to come into contact with each other
- Wash hands between handling each

17. One reason for covering food when preparing it? *(1 mark)*

To prevent dust or flies from landing on it

18. Three occasions/activities during food preparation after which you should wash your hands? *(3 marks)*

- Before and during handling food

- After using the toilet
- After handling raw eggs, meat, fish, poultry, rubbish bins, food waste, soil on vegetables
- When returning from outside the kitchen
- In between handling raw and cooked foods
- After blowing your nose or touching your mouth

19. Four food storage rules for high risk foods? *(4 marks)*

- Separate raw and cooked foods
- Wrap carefully or store in sealed containers
- Place in refrigerator or freezer as soon as possible after purchase
- Do not leave standing in a warm place for any length of time
- Refrigerate at 0°C to below 5°C
- Freeze at −18 to −24 °C
- Check door seals on refrigerators and freezers to make sure they are working properly
- Defrost refrigerators and freezers regularly
- Check and consume before the use-by date expires

20. The important temperatures and times to know for *(4 marks)*

a) cooking food: *core temperature should be 75°C or hotter for at least 2 minutes when measured with food probe*

b) keeping food hot: *core temperature should be 63°C or hotter*

c) cooling down left-over hot food: *cool to 5°C or cooler within 1½ – 2 hours*

d) re-heating left-over food: *reheat only once to a minimum of 75°C or hotter for at least 2 minutes when measured with food probe*

Chapter 7

1. Eight different factors that influence what people choose to eat? *(8 marks)*

- Health and nutrition
- Physical activity level
- Culture/tradition
- Ethics/moral beliefs/religion
- Food preferences/eating habits
- Cost
- Medical condition
- Enjoyment/celebration/occasion
- Time of day/time available to prepare and cook food
- Lifestyle
- Availability/seasonality

2. What seasonality means? *(1 mark)*

Time of year when a food crop is ready to harvest and is at its best for flavour, colour and texture and is usually cheaper and fresher

3. What food miles means? *(1 mark)*

The distance travelled by all the ingredients in a food product until it reaches consumers

4. What best-before means? *(1 mark)*

The date after which non-high risk foods will still be safe to eat but will not be at their best quality in terms of flavour, texture, appearance

5. What snacking and grazing mean? *(1 mark)*
Eating snack foods throughout the day rather than having set meal times with nothing in between

6. Four different social occasions where food plays an important part? *(4 marks)*
• Religious festivals and traditions
• Weddings
• Birthdays
• Anniversaries
• Calendar events, e.g. New Year
• Cultural festivals and traditions
• Family gatherings

7. The dietary rules for four different religions? *(4 marks)*

Buddhism Allowed: vegetarian or vegan
Not allowed: alcohol; meat and dairy foods avoided by some

Christianity Allowed: no dietary restrictions

Hinduism Allowed: vegetarian foods
Not allowed: beef, alcohol

Islam Allowed: Halal foods
Not allowed: pork, pork products and alcohol

Judaism Allowed: kosher foods; meat and dairy foods not prepared or eaten together
Not allowed: pork, shellfish

Rastafarianism
Allowed: natural and clean food, fruit, vegetables
Not allowed: pork, fish longer than 30cm

Sikhism Allowed: vegetarian foods
Not allowed: alcohol, tea, coffee (for some people)

8. Six general symptoms of food intolerance? *(6 marks)*
• Constant tiredness and weakness
• Nausea (feeling sick)
• Muscle and joint aches and pains
• Pain and bloating (gas) in the abdomen
• Diarrhoea
• Eczema and dry skin conditions

9. Three foods to avoid if a person has lactose intolerance? *(3 marks)*
Milk, yogurt, cream, cheese, butter, any food that contains dairy foods

10. Four symptoms of coeliac disease? *(4 marks)*
Anaemia, lack of energy, tiredness, weight loss, diarrhoea, poor growth in children, malnutrition

11. Four foods that coeliacs can eat? *(4 marks)*
Almonds, buckwheat, cassava, corn (maize), linseeds, millet, polenta, peas, beans, lentils, quinoa, rice, soya flour

12. Five foods that can cause food allergy? *(5 marks)*
Eggs, shellfish, fish, milk, peanuts, nuts, sesame seeds, soya, celery, celeriac, mustard, some fruits, e.g. kiwi, strawberries

13. Two symptoms of anaphylactic shock? *(2 marks)*
Swelling of mouth and throat
Difficulty swallowing, speaking or breathing

14. Six pieces of information required by law on a food label? *(6 marks)*
• The name and description of the food product
• Ingredients list (in descending order by quantity in the food)
• Net quantity (weight or volume) of the food (i.e. the amount of food you actually have to eat)
• Name and address of food manufacturer, distributor or retailer
• The place of origin of the food
• How to store, prepare and cook the product (food safety)
• The shelf-life (use-by and best before dates)
• Allergy warnings, e.g. contains milk/gluten/nuts
• Information about additives put into the food
• Nutritional information per 100g/100ml and serving quantity of the food product:
 – Energy value (kJ or kcal)
 – Protein (g)
 – Total fat (g)
 – Saturated fat (g)
 – Total carbohydrate (g)
 – Sugars (g)
 – Salt (g)

15. What nutritional information must be shown on a food label? *(7 marks)*
• Nutritional information per 100g/100ml and serving quantity of the food product:
• Energy value (kJ or kcal)
• Protein (g)
• Total fat (g)
• Saturated fat (g)
• Total carbohydrate (g)
• Sugars (g)
• Salt (g)

16. Five ways in which foods are marketed through different media? *(5 marks)*
• TV advertisements
• Internet and mobile phone advertisements and apps
• Social media
• Free samples
• Promotional leaflets
• Product placements in TV shows
• Magazines and newspapers
• Advertisement posters in the street

17. Five methods that are used to market foods? *(5 marks)*
• Price deals and special offers
• Linking a product to a celebrity or famous brand
• Healthy eating themes
• Time saving themes
• Ethical marketing

18. What pester power means? *(1 mark)*
Children pestering adults so that they buy certain food products that children have seen advertised

19. Two reasons why food labels are used? *(2 marks)*
• To give consumers information about their

product – by law and voluntarily
• To encourage consumers to buy their products

20. What marketing means? *(1 mark)*
Advertising and promoting food to consumers

Chapter 8

1. The definition of the word 'cuisine'? *(1 mark)*
A traditional style of cooking and eating that has developed in a country or region of the world

2. Two main influences on the development of cuisines? *(2 marks)*
• The local geography and climate – what can be grown in an area
• Immigration – people take their traditional cuisines with them when they move to another country

3. Three traditional things when preparing meals which different cuisines use, that makes them unique? *(3 marks)*
• Using particular ingredients grown or gathered in a local area
• Specific preparation and cooking methods
• Specific cooking equipment
• Distinctive presentation and/or serving techniques

Chapter 9

1. What the five senses are? *(5 marks)*
Smell, taste, sight, touch, sound

2. What 'appetising' means? *(1 mark)*
Food that is prepared, cooked and served so well that you want to eat it

3. What sensory descriptors are? *(1 mark)*
Words used to describe the characteristics of a food

4. How the senses of taste and smell work together? *(5 marks)*
• Flavours detected by taste buds on the tongue
• Taste buds send messages to brain about flavour
• Natural chemicals in food detected by olfactory (smell) receptors in nose
• Message sent to brain about the smell of the food
• Different areas of brain combine messages from tongue and nose to give the sensation of flavour
• 80% of flavour comes from information supplied by olfactory receptors in nose

5. What olfactory receptors are? *(1 mark)*
Special cells in nose that pick up the natural chemicals (smells/aromas) in foods

6. What taste buds are? *(1 mark)*
Special cells in the tongue that pick up the natural flavours of foods

7. Two ways in which aromas are released from foods? *(2 marks)*
• Chewing foods
• Heating foods

8. What sensory analysis is? *(1 mark)*

A way of measuring the sensory qualities of foods

9. Three different types of sensory analysis tests? *(3 marks)*

- Preference tests – which product do people like the best
- Discriminatory tests – can people tell the difference between similar food samples?
- Grading tests – to put in order a characteristic, e.g. sweetness; or the food sample people like best to worst

10. Five ways of ensuring a fair test when setting up a food tasting panel? *(5 marks)*

- It should take place in a quiet area away from food preparation and distractions
- Have between 5 and 10 tasters – they should work on their own
- Carry out test in hygienic conditions
- Give clear instructions and charts to fill in
- Tasters should drink water between samples
- Code food samples randomly
- Serve small samples and same-sized servings
- Serve samples at same temperature
- Serve on same coloured plates

Chapter 10

1. Two methods of food production? *(2 marks)*
- Intensive
- Organic
- Free range
- Hydroponic

2. What organic food production means? *(2 marks)*

Growing foods using manure, compost and natural methods of weed and pest control without chemicals

3. What hydroponic food production means? *(1 mark)*

Growing plants in water with nutrients added – not in soil

4. What intensive farming means? *(2 marks)*

Growing/rearing large numbers of the same type of plants or animals in one place

5. Three reasons why people may have concerns about the genetic modification of food? *(3 marks)*

- The possible effects of GM crops on local ecology
- Interfering with the natural process of plant and animal reproduction
- Possible allergies to foods that have been genetically modified
- Farmers may be controlled too much by the GM seed companies
- It is not possible tell a GM food from a non-GM food

6. Two advantages of eating vegetables when they are in season? *(2 marks)*

- Good flavour
- They are at their peak of freshness and nutrient content
- Often cheaper because more abundant

7. The production of which types of foods produce the most greenhouse gases? *(2 marks)*
- Dairy foods
- Meat and poultry

8. Five effects of climate change on food production? *(5 marks)*

Crops lost due to:
- Drought
- Flooding
- Damage by storms
- Forest and bush fires

Temperature changes affecting:
- What can be grown
- How well a crop grows
- Pollination by insects
- Insect and mould growth
- Livestock health
- Quality of water (often polluted)

Farming affected by:
- Loss of income if crops or livestock die
- Loss of equipment and buildings
- Loss of fertile land
- Landslides/storm damage
- Land pollution

9. What food miles means? *(1 mark)*

The distance travelled by all the ingredients in a food product until it reaches consumers

10. Three advantages of buying locally produced foods? *(3 marks)*
- Often cheaper
- No food miles – less impact on environment
- Often fresher
- Often not packaged – less impact on environment
- Available when in season

Chapter 11

1. The definition of primary processing? *(1 mark)*

Foods processed straight after harvest or slaughter to get them ready to be eaten or made into other products

2. The definition of secondary processing? *(1 mark)*

Primary processed foods are either used on their own or mixed with other foods and turned into other products

3. Four different stages of primary processing for vegetables and fruits? *(4 marks)*
- Sorting/grading
- Trimming
- Discarding unwanted ones
- Washing
- Wrapping delicate fruits
- Adding identification stickers
- Storing

4. The four different parts of a wheat grain? *(4 marks)*
- Germ
- Endosperm
- Aleurone layer
- Bran layer

5. The reasons why a meat carcase is hung for a few days after slaughter? *(3 marks)*
- To develop flavour and texture
- To help the development of lactic acid from glycogen in muscles to help preserve the meat
- To allow natural enzymes to tenderise protein and develop natural flavour

6. The reasons why milk is homogenised? *(2 marks)*
- To prevent fat (cream) from separating out and rising to the surface of the milk
- To make the texture and flavour consistent (the same) throughout

7. The reasons why milk is heat treated? *(2 marks)*
- To destroy pathogenic bacteria
- To make milk safe to drink
- To prolong the shelf-life of the milk

8. The four different types of milk available and their colour codes? *(8 marks)*
- Whole milk – blue
- Semi-skimmed milk – green
- Skimmed milk – red
- 1% milk – purple

9. The name of the wheat used to make pasta? *(1 mark)*

Durum wheat

10. Two vitamins and two minerals that are added to some foods by law? *(8 marks)*
- Vitamin A – vegetable fat spreads
- Vitamin D – vegetable fat spreads
- Vitamins B1 and B3 – wheat flour, but not wholemeal flour
- Vitamin B9 – wheat flour
- Calcium – wheat flour, but not wholemeal or self-raising flour
- Iron – wheat flour, but not wholemeal flour

11. The reasons why emulsifiers and stabilisers are added to some foods? *(2 marks)*
- To develop textures in some foods
- To prevent oil and water from separating out

12. Why preservatives are added to some foods? *(1 mark)*
- To prevent food from becoming spoiled by micro-organisms
- To increase the shelf-life of food

13. What an E number is? *(1 mark)*

A number given to a food additive that has passed safety tests and been approved for use in foods

14. The possible side effects on children of colourings added to foods? *(1 mark)*

May cause hyperactivity – unable to concentrate/temper tantrums/unable to sleep properly

15. Two reasons why nutritional modification is carried for some food products *(2 marks)*
- To make a food meet current dietary guidelines e.g. reduce sugar or salt content
- To provide a health benefit, e.g. reduce blood cholesterol levels